# Reading Stories

Bronwyn Mellor
Marnie O'Neill
Annette Patterson

# Reading
# Stories

## Activities and Texts for
## Critical Readings

National Council of Teachers of English
1111 W. Kenyon Road, Urbana, Illinois 61801-1096

Staff Editor: Thomas C. Tiller

Interior Design: Richard Maul

Cover Design: Pat Mayer

Cover Photograph: © The Stock Market/John Lund, 2000

Permissions: Kim Black

NCTE Stock Number: 39116-3050

First published in Australia in 1987 by Chalkface Press, P. O. Box 23, Cottesloe, Western Australia 6011.

©2000 by Chalkface Press.

**Library of Congress Cataloging-in-Publication Data**
Mellor, Bronwyn.
    Reading stories: activities and texts for critical readings/Bronwyn Mellor, Marnie O'Neill, Annette Patterson
        p. cm. — (NCTE Chalkface series)
"First published in Australia in 1987 by Chalkface Press"—T.p. verso.
Includes bibliographical references.
ISBN 0-8141-3911-6
    1. Readers (Secondary) 2. English language—Rhetoric—Problems, exercises, etc.
3. Reading comprehension—Problems exercises, etc. 4. Critical thinking—Problems, exercises, etc. I. O'Neill, Marnie H. II. Patterson, Annette Hinman. III. Title. IV. Series.
PE1121.M586 2000
808.3'1—dc21
                                                                        00-026234

# Series Foreword

Twenty years ago we judged the success of our students' responses to a reading assignment by the similarity of their responses to a text with ours. We saw it as our job to help students read well, to read with understanding, to read correctly; in other words, we did our best to make students read as we read. We gave little thought to the processes and experiences at work that make a single reading of a text impossible and often even undesirable. We learn much, thank goodness, as we teach. By now we have learned to encourage our students to read diversely, to recognize the processes interplaying and influencing their readings, to examine the cultural factors influencing and the cultural consequences resulting from their reading practices.

Moving beyond encouragement to effective, integrated instruction and practice is always difficult. That is why we are so excited about the NCTE Chalkface Series. Never before have we seen such practical methods of examining and understanding the personal and cultural influences that affect students' reading. The lessons actively engage students and make the invisible processes of reading explicit, demystify responses to literature, and help students understand the myriad factors influencing their reading. These books, like no other secondary reading texts we have come across, had us seeking out colleagues to share our excitement about published lessons. We now do so at every opportunity.

Among the specific strengths in the books are the inclusion of theory and of questions that provide the basis for the applications/student practices. For example, in *Literary Terms: A Practical Glossary,* the study of each term is developed as a mini-lesson, including a short piece to help students with mind-set, a brief theoretical explanation, an activity that requires application, and a summary. Some terms are very common, such as *author* and *character;* others are less common, such as *polysemy* and *poststructuralism*. The material is student-accessible; the format is somewhat different from the traditional glossaries of literary terms. Students and teachers should find the activities very useful illustrations of the terms' definitions and the theories that serve as the foundations of the study of literature.

*Gendered Fictions*, another title in the series, operates essentially from the premise that texts offer differing "versions of reality" rather than a single illustration of the real world. The authors contend that we are conditioned to make sense of text by reading from a gendered position. They offer many opportunities for students to accept or challenge particular ways of looking at masculinity or femininity. A major question proposed by the text is *how* readers read—a critical question if we want our students to be analytical readers. Perhaps equally basic, the text encourages students to look at how they become what they become. As is true of the other books, the approach is not didactic. Questioning, yes; deterministic, no.

*Reading Fictions* follows similar assumptions: texts do not have a single, definitive meaning; rather, meaning depends on a number of variables. The authors do suggest that a text may very well have a *dominant* reading (i.e., what a majority of readers may agree is there), but it may also have *alternative* readings (i.e., what other readers may believe is there). The intent is to have students look at various texts and consider what may be a dominant reading or an alternative reading. Again, the intent is to facilitate skill, not to determine what students should believe.

*Reading Hamlet* positions *Hamlet* as a revenge tragedy and provides students with a context by offering a brief look at other revenge tragedies of roughly the same period: *Thyestes, Gorboduc, The Spanish Tragedy,* and *Titus Andronicus.* That may sound overwhelming; it is, rather, illustrative and offers a genuinely effective context for the study of *Hamlet.* The text also offers a number of ways for students to study character as well as opportunities for student performance. The performance component, in particular, gives students the opportunity to be actively involved with text. The author does not assume that students have to be talented actors.

*Studying Poetry* again offers opportunities for student performance, considerations of what poetry is, and exercise in writing critiques of poetry. Poems chosen for study range from traditional to contemporary. The book strongly encourages students to identify their own favorite poems, a practice also promoted by America's current poet laureate, Robert Pinsky.

*Studying Literature* goes to the fundamental question of what makes a piece of writing "literature," asking students to consider features of writing along with their own beliefs and values and encouraging them to reflect critically on the nature of the activity in which they are engaged rather than merely engaging in it.

*Reading Stories* lays a firm foundation for students moving toward becoming critical readers. From exploring their own expectations prior to reading a work (or rereading one) to questioning authorial intent to exploring cultural and social assumptions, this book makes explicit both the ways in which readings are constructed and the bases on which students might choose among them.

*Investigating Texts* builds on that foundation by exploring the deeper questions of how texts are made, how ways of reading change, and how texts can be read differently. As in all the books, numerous activities are provided to facilitate such exploration and application, promoting student interaction, an active relationship with the texts provided and, by extension, an active relationship with new texts they encounter.

We are delighted that NCTE has arranged to make Chalkface books available to its members. We are confident that teachers will share our enthusiasm for the publications.

Richard Luckert
Olathe East High School
Olathe, Kansas

William G. McBride
Colorado State University
Fort Collins

# Contents

# Acknowledgments

We gratefully acknowledge Jane Leggett and Elisabeth Plackett for their contribution to the work on "Turned" and "The Great Leapfrog Contest," respectively. We also acknowledge the help of the following persons in the development of this book: Lynne Carew, Gary Davidson, Daphne Denaro, Elaine Forrestal, Derryn Hammond, Judith Hemming, Philippa Hunt, Betty Johnson, Ros Moger, Jo-Anne Reid, Mike Raleigh, John Richmond, Helen Savva, and Michael Simons.

We thank Peter Forrestal for his invaluable assistance in editing the manuscript, and Barbara North and Zan Blair for typing it.

# Introduction

*Reading Stories* is an anthology of short stories and ways of reading those stories. The readings of the stories presented here are not intended to be definitive; we would argue that there are many possible readings for any given story. Our concern is not so much with "meaning" as with the processes and production of meaning through various approaches to a text. Rather than ask the question, "What is the meaning of the story?" we ask, "How is the story asking to be read?"

In developing this book, we began with the idea that readers should be encouraged to reflect on the nature of the activity in which they are engaged. Given that students spend a lot of time listening to and reading stories—and have an enormous knowledge of them—we wanted to ask students quite explicitly to think about the nature of stories and especially about their reading of them.

*Before* reading a story, we wanted students to ask such questions as: What expectations do I have of this story? Where do these expectations come from?

*While* reading we wanted them to ask: How am I being asked to read this text? How is this invitation phrased? How am I, in fact, reading it? Could it be read otherwise?

In short, we wanted to encourage students to confront the reading the text invites and to explore its construction and its ideology. We assumed that:

◼ the starting point for any discussion about a piece of literature is the fact that it is a deliberate construction or "artifact";

◼ a text does not emerge from a timeless, placeless zone but is produced *and read* in a particular cultural, social, and historical context;

◼ literary texts carry assumptions and attitudes and convey messages—not all of which may be intended or meant by the writer.

These assumptions led us to a concern that is central to our approach, and that is our focus on the representation of gender, class, and race in literary texts.

Essentially, we wanted to promote in students a greater consciousness of the processes involved in writing and reading and a concern with the ideological nature of literary texts.

## To the Teacher

This text consists of five sections; the first four are intended to offer a cumulative learning experience, with each section assuming a knowledge and experience of the terms and concepts encountered in the preceding sections. For this reason, it is suggested that these four sections should be used in sequence, although the emphasis teachers decide to give to the various sections may vary. In Section 5, fewer activities have been planned around the stories, on the assumption that students will bring to the readings the knowledge and strategies acquired in working through the first four sections.

Within each section, many of the activities are planned for pairs or small groups, which may then lead to whole class sharing or individual writing. In pragmatic terms, the pairs and small groups allow more students to talk or participate actively more of the time. However, it is also assumed that it is in the small groups that students are more likely to articulate their responses, offer tentative hypotheses, and interrogate the text and each other about their interpretations. Emphasis is placed on the value of sharing information and responses and examining critically some of the ideas developed in small groups in the arena of whole class discussion. We also appreciate the value of individual writing in helping students consolidate and control ideas that may have been generated in the flux of small group or whole class discussion. Obviously, different classes work in different ways, and you will want to vary the proportion of individual, small group, and whole class activities to suit the needs of your particular students.

Since many of the concepts presented in the book are abstract and may be unfamiliar to students, we have deliberately developed a number of extremely concrete activities such as chart building, time lines, and semantic differentials. We see these as a means of getting ideas down on paper so that they can be discussed and challenged. Your students may be able to come to terms with abstractions without working through all of the concrete tasks; you may want to leave some things out, or substitute others that will achieve the same objectives in ways more appropriate to your students.

In cases where predictions or deletions are used to help students explore their readings, it will be worthwhile to consider how to present the stories in ways that encourage students to give adequate time to the suggested activities before continuing reading.

We have tried not to take a didactic or moralistic approach to the stories in the presentation of the materials. We hope that by working through the stages in this book students will find themselves considering and possibly reevaluating the content and ideology of what they read, as well as considering issues which may previously have been taken for granted. Some of the material may imply a critical stance toward the ideology reflected in some of the stories—but we have tried to suggest a variety of strategies which encourage students to explore the stories and their readings of them for themselves.

# 1 Expectations

- What expectations do readers have of stories?
- Where do readers' expectations come from?
- Can a story ask to be read in a particular way?
- Do readers read a story in the same way the second, third, or fourth time?
- Can stories have "messages"?

## "The Good Corn" and "Turned"

Both stories in this section explore the relationships between one male and two female characters. "The Good Corn" was written by the English author H. E. Bates in 1951, and "Turned" was written by Charlotte Perkins Gilman in the United States in 1911. The accompanying activities are designed to help you think about your readings of "The Good Corn" and "Turned" and to explore the following considerations:

- the expectations you have of these two short stories;
- your ability to predict much of what happens in them.

You are also asked to consider—in some detail—what happens when readers' expectations are challenged. For example:

- What effect can it have on how we read?
- What happens to the story and its "messages"?

## "The Good Corn"

In "The Good Corn" one of the women is a middle-aged wife, the other a younger woman who has come to work on the farm owned by the married woman and her husband. You may have begun already to form expectations about a story involving these three characters. In your pairs or groups, spend a few minutes listing ideas of what "The Good Corn" could be about.

# The Good Corn

*H. E. Bates*

For twenty-five years Joe Mortimer and his wife had lived in a valley, getting a living from raising hens and geese, a few cows and calves, the fruit from half a dozen cherry trees and an acre or two of corn.[1]

Their small red brick house, surrounded by coops of wire and low wooden sheds for chickens, stood close to a railway line, and occasionally passengers could look out and see, walking about the small grass paddock or across the bare autumn stubbles, a woman with wispy fair hair and long brown arms. Sometimes she was lovingly leading a calf by a halter; sometimes she seemed to be earnestly talking to flocks of geese and hens. At times a man was with her: a tall gaunt-framed man with close-cut hair and spare knotty muscles and water-blue eyes that slowly lifted themselves and gazed absently on the windows of passing trains. In summer there were always many children on the trains, eagerly pressing faces to the glass as they travelled down to the sea, and whenever the Mortimers caught sight of them there was a sudden brightness on their faces, a great eagerness, almost an illumination, as they smiled and waved their hands.

Every Tuesday and again on Saturday the Mortimers drove in a small black truck to market. They took with them cases of eggs, half a dozen unplucked brown chickens, a few chips of cherries in their season and odd things like bunches of turnips and onions, a brace of pigeons, a hare and daffodils carefully tied in dozens.

In the evenings, when they came home again, they counted out their money on the kitchen table. They laid it out in little piles of silver and copper and notes, counting it several times to make sure how much they had.

Then when the counting was finished Joe Mortimer would divide the money exactly in half. Solemnly, from the very beginning of their marriage, he would put one half into a tin cash box and then push the other across to his wife, who took it from him with long, uneager hands.

"You know what that's for," he would say, "put that away."

At first they were quite sure about children. It seemed as natural to think of children coming as to think of eggs in the hen-runs and calves for cows and flowers on cherry trees. It was merely a question of time before children came. Mrs. Mortimer thought of children laughing and running among flocks of hens, scattering grain, tossing it among the snapping, quarrelling brown feathers. In early spring in cold wet weather, she sometimes nursed the first yellow chicks in warm flannel, in baskets, under the kitchen stove. That was the sort of thing children always loved, she thought.

It was in summer, when the corn was ready, that Mortimer thought of them most. In imagination he saw boys riding in harvest carts or chasing rabbits among shocks

---

1. In its general sense, *corn* refers to various cereal grasses, including wheat, oats, and (in the United States) sweet corn. In England, where Bates lived, the term refers to wheat.

of wheat and barley. He saw himself cutting them ash-plants from hedgerows or teaching them to thresh wheat in the palms of their hands. He saw them bouncing on piles of fresh light straw on threshing days.

Then gradually, as time went by and there were no children, he became resigned to it in a puzzled, absent sort of way. It did not embitter him. If there were no children there were no children, he thought. That was nature; that was how it was. You could not alter that. It turned out like that with some people. There was nothing you could do about it but hope and make the best of it.

But his wife could not see it like that. It was not simply that she wanted children; it was not merely a question of pride. It was a woman's duty to have children; it was all of a woman's life to give birth. Not to bear children, when her pride was deep, was something more to a woman than misfortune. It was a failure in her living. It was like a hen that did not lay eggs or a cow that was sterile or a tree that never came into blossom. There was no point in the existence of them.

As time went on she drew more and more into herself. With something more than injured pride she drew deep down into an isolation where she thought of nothing but the failure that came from sterility. The reproach of failure never left her; she could not grow used to the pain of it. It was like a gnawing physical disability, an ugly mark she wanted to hide.

All the time, waiting for children, the two of them worked very hard. They saved money. Chickens and eggs went to market every week; cherries brought good money in summer; there was always enough corn for the hens and enough hay for the cows and calves and plenty over.

Whenever a new calf came she cried a little. The mournful tender glassiness of a cow's big eyes after birth was something she could not bear. She liked to lift the soft wet heads of the new calves and hold them in her arms. She liked the smell of milk on their faces and the gluey suck of their mouths if she fed them from the bucket.

After they had been married twenty-five years she stood one morning in the small cow-shed at the back of the house and watched a calf die in her arms. It was a red heifer calf and she began to cry bitterly. The calf had been dropped in the meadow the previous afternoon, prematurely, while she and Mortimer were at market. A cold wet wind with hail in it was blowing from the west. The calf could not stand on its feet by the time she and Mortimer found it and there was a drift of wet hail along the side of its body.

She went on to grieve about the calf. The death of the calf became a personal thing. She found she could not sleep at night. She bit the edges of the pillow so that she could lay and cry without a sound. After a time there was a continuous pain in her chest: a great bony bolt that shot across her throat and made it difficult to swallow.

At the same time she began to despise herself.

"Don't come near me. I'm no good to you. You should have found someone else, not me. What have I done for you? What good have I ever been?"

"Don't say that. Don't talk like that," Mortimer said. "You're not well. You're not yourself. I'm going to get the doctor to look at you."

The doctor spent a long time with her in the bedroom, alone, sitting on the edge of the bed, asking questions. She stared at him most of the time with pallid, boring eyes. After a time he went downstairs and gave Mortimer a pipe of tobacco and walked about the yard, among the crying geese, and talked to him.

"All she can talk about is how she's been no good to me," Joe said. "How I'm not to go near her. How she hates herself. How she's been a failure all the time."

The doctor did not answer; the geese cried and squawked among the barns.

"Neither of us is sleeping well," Joe said. "I can't put up with it. I can't stand it much longer."

"Was there something that began it?"

"The calf. We lost a calf about three weeks ago. She blamed herself for that."

"Never thought of going away from here?" the doctor said.

"Away?"

"How long have you lived here?"

"Five and twenty years. Nearly six and twenty."

"I believe you might do well to move," the doctor said.

"Move? Where to? What for?"

"It might be that everything here has the same association. This is where she wanted her children and this is where she never had them. She might be happier if you moved away from here."

"She misses children. She'd have been all right with children," Joe said.

"Think it over," the doctor said. "She needs a rest too. Get her to take it a little easier. Get a girl to help in the kitchen and with the hens. It'll be company for her. Perhaps she won't think of herself so much."

"All right. It upsets me to see her break her heart like that."

"I wish I were a farmer. If I were a farmer you know what I'd like to do?" the doctor said. "Grow nothing but corn. That's life. Give up practically everything but corn. With the cows and stock and birds it's all day and every day. But with corn you go away and you come back and your corn's still there. It's a wonderful thing, corn. That's what I'd like to do. There's something marvellous about corn."

The following spring they moved to a farm some distance up the hill. All their married lives they had lived on flat land, with no view except the hedges of their own fields and a shining stretch of railway line. Now they found themselves with land that ran away on a gentle slope, with a view below it of an entire broad valley across which trains ran like smoking toys.

The girl who answered their advertisement for help was short and dark, with rather sleepy brown eyes, a thick bright complexion and rosy-knuckled hands. She called at the house with her mother, who did most of what talking there was.

"She's been a bit off colour. But she's better now. She wants to work in the fresh air for a bit. You want to work in the fresh air don't you, Elsie?"

"Yes," Elsie said.

"She's very quiet, but she'll get used to you," her mother said. "She don't say much, but she'll get used to you. She's not particular either. You're not particular, are you, Elsie?"

"No," Elsie said.

"She's a good girl. She won't give no trouble," her mother said.

"How old is she?" Mortimer said.

"Eighteen," her mother said. "Eighteen and in her nineteen. She'll be nineteen next birthday, won't you, Elsie?"

"Yes," Elsie said.

The girl settled into the house and moved about it with unobtrusive quietness. As she stood at the kitchen sink, staring down across the farm-yard, at the greening hedgerows of hawthorn and the rising fields of corn, she let her big-knuckled fingers wander dreamily over the wet surface of the dishes as if she were a blind person trying to trace a pattern. Her brown eyes travelled over the fields as if she were searching for something she had lost there.

Something about this lost and dreamy attitude gradually began to puzzle Mrs. Mortimer. She saw in the staring brown eyes an expression that reminded her of the glazed eyes of the calf.

"You won't get lonely up here, will you?" she said. "I don't want you to get lonely."

"No," the girl said.

"You tell me if you get anyways lonely, won't you?"

"Yes."

"I want you to feel happy here," Mrs. Mortimer said. "I want you to feel as if you was one of our own."

As the summer went on the presence of the girl seemed occasionally to comfort Mrs. Mortimer. Sometimes she was a little more content; she did not despise herself so much. During daytime at least she could look out on new fields, over new distances, and almost persuade herself that what she saw was a different sky. But at night, in darkness, the gnaw of self-reproaches remained. She could not prevent the old cry from breaking out:

"Don't come near me. Not yet. Soon perhaps—but not yet. Not until I feel better about things. I will one day, but not yet."

Once or twice she even cried: "You could get someone else. I wouldn't mind. I honestly wouldn't mind. It's hard for you I know it is. I wouldn't mind."

Sometimes Mortimer, distracted too, got up and walked about the yard in summer darkness, smoking hard, staring at the summer stars.

All summer, in the afternoons, after she had worked in the house all morning, the girl helped about the yard and the fields. By July the corn was level as a mat of thick blue-green pile between hedgerows of wild rose and blackberry flower. In the garden in front of the house bushes of currant were bright with berries that glistened like scarlet pearls from under old lace curtains.

The thick fingers of the girl were stained red with the juice of currants as she gathered them. Her finger marks were bright smears across the heavy front of her cotton pinafore.

As the two women knelt among the bushes, in alley-ways of ripe fruit, lifting the bleached creamy curtains in the July sun, Mrs. Mortimer said:

"I'm glad of another pair of hands. I don't know what I should have done without another pair of hands. Your mother will miss you back home I reckon."

"She's got six more to help," the girl said. "She don't need me all that much."

"Six. Not children?"

"When I was home there was seven. Eight before the baby went."

"Before the baby went? Whose baby? What happened to the baby?"

"It was mine. I gave it away," the girl said. "I didn't know what to do with it no sense, so I gave it away. My sister adopted it. They all said it was best like that. I gave it to my married sister."

"Gave it away?" Mrs. Mortimer sat on the earth, between the bushes, feeling sick. "Gave it away? A baby? You gave it away?"

"Yes," Elsie said. "It's no bother to me now."

Towards the end of the month the first corn began to ripen. The sheen of olive on the wheat began to turn pale yellow, then to the colour of fresh-baked crust on bread.

As he looked at it Mortimer remembered what the doctor had said. "You go away and you come back and your corn's still there. It's a wonderful thing, corn. There's something marvellous about corn."

Now as he looked at it he could not help feeling proud of the corn. It helped him too as he thought of his wife. It hurt him to hear her cry that he must keep away from her, that the pride in her was still tortured, the love in her not smoothed out. The corn helped to soothe him a little. The wind that ran darkly across it on cloudy days had a beautiful twist as if long snakes were slipping among the ears.

In the evenings, after supper, while the two women washed the dishes, he was often alone with the corn. And one evening as he stood watching it he did something he had always liked to do. He broke off an ear and began to thresh it in his hands, breaking the husk from the grain with the pressure of the balls of his thumbs.

While he was still doing this the girl came down the hillside from the house with a message that a man had called to deliver a sailcloth. Mortimer blew on the grain that lay in his cupped hands, scattering a dancing cloud of chaff like summer flies.

"I'll be up in a minute," he said. "Here tell me what you think of that."

"The wheat?" she said.

She picked a few grains of wheat from the palm of his hand. She did not toss them into her mouth but put them in one by one, with the tips of her fingers, biting them with the front of her teeth. Her teeth were surprisingly level and white and he could see the whiteness of the new grains on her tongue as she bit them.

"They're milky," she said.

"Still want a few more days, I think," he said.

As they walked back up the field she plucked an ear of wheat as high as the girl herself, and rustled it in her fingers. When she bent down to blow on the husks a small gust of wind suddenly turned and blew the chaff up into her face. She laughed rather loudly, showing her teeth again, and he said:

"Here, you want to do it like this. You want to bring your thumbs over so that you can blow down there and make a chimney."

"How?" she said.

A moment later he was holding her hands. He stood slightly behind her and held her hands and showed her how to cup them so that the chaff could blow out through the chimney made by her fingers.

"Now blow," he said.

"I can't blow for laughing."

Her mouth spluttered and a new gust of laughter blew into her hands and a dancing cloud of chaff leapt up in a spurt from her fingers. She laughed again and he felt her body shaking. A few husks of wheat blew into her mouth and a few more stuck to the moist edges of her lips as she laughed.

She pulled out her handkerchief to wipe her lips, still laughing, and suddenly he found himself trying to help her and then in a clumsy way was trying to kiss her face and mouth at the same time.

"Elsie," he said. "Here, Elsie——."

She laughed again and said, "We don't want to fool here. Somebody will see us if we start fooling here. Mrs. Mortimer will see us. Not here."

"You were always so quiet," he said.

"It isn't always the loud ones who say most, is it?" she said. She began to shake herself. "Now I've got chaff down my neck. Look at me."

She laughed again and shook herself, twisting her body in a way that suddenly reminded him of the twist of dark air running among the ripening corn. He tried to kiss her again and she said:

"Not here I keep telling you. Sometime if you like but not here. Not in broad daylight. I don't like people watching me."

"All right."

"Some other time. It's so public here," she said. "There'll be another time."

By the end of August the corn was cut and carted. The stubbles were empty except for the girl and Mrs. Mortimer, gleaning on fine afternoons, and a few brown hens scratching among the straw. "I could never quite give up the hens," Mrs. Mortimer said. "It would be an awful wrench to give them up. I didn't mind the cherries and I didn't even mind the calves so much. But the hens are company. I can talk to the hens."

About the house, in the yard, bright yellow stacks stood ready for threshing, and there was a fresh clean smell of straw on the air. During summer the face of the girl had reddened with sun and air and as autumn came on it seemed to broaden and flatten, the thick skin ripe and healthy in texture.

"Soon be winter coming on, Elsie," Mrs. Mortimer said. "You think you'll stay up here with us for the winter?"

"Well, I expect I shall if nothing happens," Elsie said.

"Happens? If what happens?"

"Well, you never know what may happen," Elsie said, "do you?"

"I want you to stay if you can," Mrs. Mortimer said. "They get a lot of snow up here some winters, but perhaps we'll be lucky. Stay if you can. I got now so as I think of you as one of our own."

In a growing fondness for the girl Mrs. Mortimer occasionally remembered and reflected on the incident of the baby. It was very strange and inexplicable to her, the incident of the baby. It filled her with mystery and wonder. It was a mystery beyond comprehension that a girl could conceive and bear a child and then, having delivered it, give it away. She felt she would never be able to grasp the reasons for that. "You'd think it would be like tearing your own heart out to do a thing like that," she thought.

Towards the end of November the first snow fell, covering the hillsides down to within a hundred feet of the valley. The house stood almost on the dividing line of snow, like a boat at the edge of a tide, between fields that were still fresh green with winter corn and others smooth with the first thin white fall.

"I've got something to tell you," the girl said to Mrs. Mortimer. "I don't think I'll be staying here much longer."

"Not staying."

"No."

"Why not?"

"I don't think I will, that's all."

"Is it the snow? You don't like the snow, do you? That's what it is, the snow."

"It's not the snow so much."

"Is it us then?" Mrs. Mortimer said. "Don't you like us no more?"

"I like you. It isn't that," the girl said.

"What is it then, Elsie? Don't say you'll go. What is it?"

"It's the baby," Elsie said.

"The baby?" Mrs. Mortimer felt a pain of tears in her eyes. "I somehow thought one day you'd want it back. I'm glad."

"Not that baby," the girl said. "Not that one. I'm going to have another."

Mrs. Mortimer felt a strange sense of disturbance. She was shaken once again by disbelief and pain. She could not speak and the girl said:

"In the Spring. April I think it'll be."

"How did you come to do that ?" Mrs. Mortimer said. She spoke quietly, almost to herself. She thought, with the old pain, of her years of sterility. She remembered how, in distraction, she had so much despised herself, how she had turned, out of pride, into isolation, away from Joe. "I don't understand," she said.

At night she turned restlessly in her bed. Splinters of moonlight between the edges of the curtains cut across her eyes and kept them stiffly open.

"Can't you sleep again?" Joe said.

"It's the girl," she said. "Elsie. I can't get her out of my mind."

"What's wrong with Elsie?"

"She's having another baby," she said. "In the Spring."

"Oh, no!" he said. "Oh! No. No. You don't mean that? No."

"It seems she got to know somebody. Somehow," she said. She felt across her eyes the hard stab of moonlight. She turned and put her hand out and touched Joe on the shoulder. "Joe," she said. "That doesn't seem right, does it? It doesn't seem fair."

Joe did not answer.

"It doesn't seem fair. It's not right. It seems cruel," she said.

The following night she could not sleep again. She heard a westerly wind from across the valley beating light squalls of rain on the windows of the bedroom. The air was mild in a sudden change and she lay with her arms outside the coverlet, listening to the rain washing away the snow.

Suddenly Joe took hold of her hands and began crying into them.

"I didn't know what I was doing. She kept asking me. It was her who kept asking me."

She could not speak and he turned his face to the pillow.

"I didn't think you wanted me. You used to say so. I got so as I thought you didn't want me any more. You used to say—."

"I want you," she said. "Don't be afraid of that."

"Did she say anything?" he said. "Did she say it was me?"

"No. She didn't say."

"Did you think it was me?"

"I'd begun to think," she said. "I thought I could tell by the way you couldn't look at her."

She heard him draw his breath in dry snatches, unable to find words. Suddenly she was sorry for him, with no anger or reproach or bitterness, and she stretched out her long bare arms.

"Come here to me," she said. "Come close to me. I'm sorry. It was me. It was my fault."

"Never," he said. "Never. I won't have that—."

"Listen to me," she said. "Listen to what I say."

As she spoke she was aware of a feeling of being uplifted, of a depressive weight being taken from her.

"Listen, Joe, if I ask her perhaps she'll give it to us. You remember? She gave the other away."

"No," he said. "You couldn't do that—."

"I could," she said. She began smiling to herself in the darkness. "Tomorrow I'll ask her. We could do it properly—so that it was ours."

"If you forgive me," Joe said. "Only if you do that—."

"I forgive you," she said.

She went through the rest of the winter as if she were carrying the baby herself. "You mustn't do that, Elsie. Don't lift that," she would say: "Take a lie down for an hour. Rest yourself—it'll do you the world of good to rest." She looked forward to Spring with a strange acute sensation of being poised on a wire, frightened that she would fall before she got there.

When the baby was born she wrapped it in a warm blanket and succoured it like the early chicken she had once wrapped in flannel, in a basket, under the stove.

"And I can have him?" she said. "You haven't changed your mind? You won't change your mind, will you?"

"No," the girl said. "You can have him. I don't want the bother. You can look after him."

"We'll love him," she said. "We'll look after him."

On a day in late April she took the baby and carried him down through the yard, in the sunshine, to where the fields began. Hedgerows were breaking everywhere into bright new leaf. Primroses lay in thick pale drifts under the shelter of them and under clumps of ash and hornbeam. In every turn of wind there was a whitening of anemones, with cowslips trembling gold about the pasture.

She lifted the baby up, in the sunshine, against the blue spring sky, and laughed and shook him gently, showing him the world of leaf and corn.

"Look at all the flowers!" she said. "Look at the corn! The corn looks good, doesn't it? It's going to be good this year, isn't it? Look at it all!—isn't the corn beautiful?"

High above her, on the hill, there was a sound of endless lark song and in the fields the young curved lines of corn were wonderfully fresh and trembling in the sun.

## Expectations and Predictions

How much of the story did you predict correctly?

■ With your partners or in your groups, go through the list of ideas you noted down before reading "The Good Corn" and put a check by those predictions that turned out to be accurate, or nearly so.

Before reading a story or a novel, we almost always have expectations about the kind of story we are going to read, and we make predictions about it. Sometimes our expectations are not met, and we feel disappointed. There are times, however, when we can be pleasantly surprised by the challenge to our expectations.

### How Do Readers Make Predictions?

Prior to reading "The Good Corn" you were given only a little information about the story. You were told the title, the setting of the story, and the gender and approximate ages of the characters and their relationships with each other.

■ In your pairs or groups, talk about each of the pieces of prereading information and assess:

1. how useful each was in enabling you to make predictions;
2. what kind of ideas each piece of information suggested;
3. where these ideas "came from."

■ Make notes of your findings in a format similar to the one below.

|  | Information Given | How Useful in Making Predictions? | Kind of Ideas Suggested? | Origin of Ideas? |
|---|---|---|---|---|
| The title |  |  |  |  |
| Setting |  |  |  |  |
| Characters |  |  |  |  |

## Characters

In your groups or pairs, describe your reactions to the three main characters in "The Good Corn":

- ■ Spend a few minutes talking about your reactions to Elsie, Mrs. Mortimer, and Joe Mortimer.
- ■ Draw up a chart similar to the one below and make a list of four or five adjectives to describe each character under his or her name.
- ■ Compare your lists with other groups in your class, making any appropriate additions or changes to your original lists.

| Mrs. Mortimer | Joe Mortimer | Elsie |
|---|---|---|
|  |  |  |

- ■ Keep your final lists in your file or folder as you will be asked to refer to them later in the chapter.

# "Turned"

Like "The Good Corn," the next story, "Turned," features two women and one man as the main characters. The story has been divided into several passages. At the end of each passage you are asked, in your groups, to reflect upon what you have just read and to predict what will happen next. As you will be asked to share your reflections and predictions at the end of Passage 7, you will need to make very brief notes of your reflections during the first half of the story.

## Turned _____

*Charlotte Perkins Gilman*

## Passage 1

In her soft carpeted, thick curtained, richly furnished chamber, Mrs. Marroner lay sobbing on the wide, soft bed.

She sobbed bitterly, chokingly, despairingly; her shoulders heaved and shook convulsively; her hands were tight clenched. She had forgotten her elaborate dress, the more elaborate bed-cover; forgotten her dignity, her self control, her pride. In her mind was an overwhelming, unbelievable horror, an immeasurable loss, a turbulent, struggling mass of emotion.

In her reserved, superior, Boston-bred life, she had never dreamed that it would be possible for her to feel so many things at once, and with such trampling intensity.

She tried to cool her feelings into thoughts; to stiffen them into words; to control herself—and could not. It brought vaguely to her mind an awful moment in the breakers at York Beach, one summer in girlhood when she had been swimming under water and could not find the top.

- ■ What do you learn about Mrs. Marroner from this passage?
- ■ What sort of emotions is she experiencing?
- ■ Can you guess at what might have caused them?

## Passage 2

In her uncarpeted, thin-curtained, poorly furnished chamber on the top floor, Gerta Petersen lay sobbing on the narrow, hard bed.

She was a larger frame than her mistress, grandly built and strong; but all her proud young womanhood was prostrate now, convulsed with agony, dissolved in tears. She did not try to control herself. She wept for two.

- ■ What do you learn about Gerta Petersen from this passage?
- ■ Can you guess why she is feeling as she is?
- ■ What do you think "She wept for two" might mean?

## Passage 3

If Mrs. Marroner suffered more from the wreck and ruin of a longer love—perhaps a deeper one; if her tastes were finer, her ideals loftier; if she bore the pangs of bitter jealousy and outraged pride, Gerta had personal shame to meet, a hopeless future, and a looming present which filled her with unreasoning terror.

She had come like a meek young goddess into that perfectly ordered house, strong, beautiful, full of goodwill and eager obedience, but ignorant and childish—a girl of eighteen.

Mr. Marroner had frankly admired her, and so had his wife. They discussed her visible perfections and as visible limitations with that perfect confidence which they had so long enjoyed. Mrs. Marroner was not a jealous woman. She had never been jealous in her life—till now.

Gerta had stayed and learned their ways. They had both been fond of her. Even the cook was fond of her. She was what is called "willing," was unusually teachable and plastic; and Mrs. Marroner, with her early habits of giving instruction, tried to educate her somewhat.

"I never saw anyone so docile," Mrs. Marroner had often commented. "It is perfection in a servant, but almost a defect in character. She is so helpless and confiding."

She was precisely that: a tall, rosy-cheeked baby; rich womanhood without, helpless infancy within. Her braided wealth of dead-gold hair, her grave blue eyes, her mighty shoulders and long, firmly molded limbs seemed those of a primal earth spirit; but she was only an ignorant child, with a child's weakness.

When Mr. Marroner had to go abroad for his firm, unwillingly, hating to leave his wife, he told her he felt quite safe to leave her in Gerta's hands—she would take care of her.

"Be good to your mistress, Gerta," he told the girl that last morning at breakfast. "I leave her to you to take care of. I shall be back in a month at latest."

Then he turned, smiling, to his wife. "And you must take care of Gerta , too," he said. "I expect you'll have her ready for college when I get back."

This was seven months ago. Business had delayed him from week to week, from month to month. He wrote to his wife, long, loving, frequent letters, deeply regretting the delay, explaining how necessary, how profitable it was, congratulating her on the wide resources she had, her well-filled, well-balanced mind, her many interests.

"If I should be eliminated from your scheme of things, by any of those 'acts of God' mentioned on the tickets, I do not feel that you would be an utter wreck," he said. "That is very comforting to me. Your life is so rich and wide that no loss, even a great one, would wholly cripple you. But nothing of the sort is likely to happen, and I shall be home again in three weeks—if this thing gets settled. And you will be looking so lovely, with that eager light in your eyes and the changing flush I know so well—and love so well! My dear wife! We shall have to have a new honeymoon— other moons come every month, why shouldn't the mellifluous kind?"

He often asked after "little Gerta," sometimes enclosed a picture postcard to her, joked with his wife about her laborious efforts to educate "the child," was so loving and merry and wise—

All this was racing through Mrs. Marroner's mind as she lay there with the broad, hemstitched border of fine linen sheeting crushed and twisted in one hand, and the other holding a sodden handkerchief.

■ What more do you learn about Mrs. Marroner and Gerta?
■ What do you learn about the relationship between Mr. Marroner and his wife and the relationship between Mr. Marroner and Gerta?
■ Chronologically this passage takes place before the first two passages; it is a flashback. What might this tell you about how the rest of the story could be organized?

## Passage 4

She had tried to teach Gerta, and had grown to love the patient, sweet-natured child, in spite of her dullness. At work with her hands, she was clever, if not quick, and could keep small accounts from week to week. But to the woman who held a Ph.D., who had been on the faculty of a college, it was like baby-tending.

Perhaps having no babies of her own made her love the big child the more, though the years between them were but fifteen.

To the girl she seemed quite old, of course; and her young heart was full of grateful affection for the patient care which made her feel so much at home in this new land.

And then she had noticed a shadow on the girl's bright face. She looked nervous, anxious, worried. When the bell rang, she seemed startled, would rush hurriedly to the door. Her peals of frank laughter no longer rose from the area gate as she stood talking with the always admiring tradesmen.

Mrs. Marroner had labored long to teach her more reserve with men, and flattered herself that her words were at last effective. She suspected the girl of homesickness, which was denied. She suspected her of illness, which was denied also. At last she suspected her of something which could not be denied.

For a long time she refused to believe it, waiting. Then she had to believe it, but schooled herself to patience and understanding. "The poor child," she said. "She is here without a mother—she is so foolish and yielding—I must not be too stern with her." And she tried to win the girl's confidence with wise, kind words.

But Gerta had literally thrown herself at her feet and begged her with streaming tears not to turn her away. She would admit nothing, explain nothing, but frantically promised to work for Mrs. Marroner as long as she lived—if only she would keep her.

■ What is Mrs. Marroner going to do and what reasons may she have for doing so?

## Passage 5

Revolving the problem carefully in her mind, Mrs. Marroner thought she would keep her, at least for the present. She tried to repress her sense of ingratitude in one she had so sincerely tried to help, and the cold, contemptuous anger she had always felt for such weakness.

"The thing to do now," she said to herself, "is to see her through this safely. The child's life should not be hurt any more than is unavoidable. I will ask Dr. Bleet about it—what a comfort a woman doctor is! I'll stand by the poor, foolish thing till it's over, and then get her back to Sweden somehow with her baby. How they do come where they are not wanted—and don't come where they are wanted!" And Mrs. Marroner, sitting alone in the quiet, spacious beauty of the house, almost envied Gerta.

Then came the deluge.

She had sent the girl out for needed air toward dark. The late mail came; she took it in herself. One letter for her—her husband's letter. She knew the postmark, the stamp, the kind of typewriting. She impulsively kissed it in the dim hall. No one would suspect Mrs. Marroner of kissing her husband's letters—but she did, often.

She looked over the others. One was for Gerta, and not from Sweden. It looked precisely like her own. This struck her as a little odd, but Mr. Marroner had several times sent messages and cards to the girl. She laid the letter on the hall table and took hers to her room.

- ◼ Why does Mrs. Marroner think Gerta's letter a little odd?
- ◼ What do you think her letter contains?
- ◼ Can you guess at what Gerta's letter contains?

## Passage 6

"My poor child," it began. What letter of hers had been sad enough to warrant that?

"I am deeply concerned at the news you send." What news to so concern him had she written? "You must bear it bravely, little girl. I shall be home soon, and will take care of you, of course. I hope there is no immediate anxiety—you do not say. Here is money, in case you need it. I expect to get home in a month at latest. If you have to go, be sure to leave your address at my office. Cheer up—be brave—I will take care of you."

The letter was typewritten, which was not unusual. It was unsigned, which was unusual. It enclosed an American bill—fifty dollars. It did not seem in the least like any letter she had ever had from her husband, or any letter she could imagine him writing. But a strange, cold feeling was creeping over her, like a flood rising around the house.

She utterly refused to admit the ideas which began to bob and push about outside her mind, and to force themselves in. Yet under the pressure of these repudiated thoughts she went downstairs and brought up the other letter—the one to Gerta. She laid them side by side on a smooth dark space on the table; marched to the piano and played, with stern precision, refusing to think, till the girl came back. When she came in, Mrs. Marroner rose quietly and came to the table. "Here is a letter for you," she said.

The girl stepped forward eagerly, saw the two lying together there, hesitated, and looked at her mistress.

"Take yours, Gerta. Open it please."

The girl turned frightened eyes upon her.

"I want you to read it, here," said Mrs. Marroner.

"Oh, ma'am—No! Please don't make me!"

"Why not?"

There seemed to be no reason at hand, and Gerta flushed more deeply and opened her letter. It was long; it was evidently puzzling to her; it began "My Dear Wife." She read slowly.

"Are you sure it is your letter?" asked Mrs. Marroner. "Is not this one yours? Is not that one—mine?"

She held out the other letter to her.

"It is a mistake," Mrs. Marroner went on, with a hard quietness. She had lost her social bearings somehow, lost her usual keen sense of the proper thing to do. This was not life; this was nightmare.

"Do you not see? Your letter was put in my envelope and my letter was put in your envelope. Now we understand it."

But poor Gerta had no antechamber to her mind, no trained forces to preserve order while agony entered. The thing swept over her, resistless, overwhelming. She cowered before the outraged wrath she expected; and from some hidden cavern that wrath arose and swept over her in pale flame.

■ What is Mrs. Marroner going to say and do now?

## Passage 7

"Go and pack your trunk," said Mrs. Marroner. "You will leave my house tonight. Here is your money."

She laid down the fifty-dollar bill. She put with it a month's wages. She had no shadow of pity for those anguished eyes, those tears which she heard drop on the floor.

"Go to your room and pack," said Mrs. Marroner. And Gerta, always obedient, went.

Then Mrs. Marroner went to hers, and spent a time she never counted, lying on her face on the bed.

But the training of the twenty-eight years which had elapsed before her marriage; the life at college, both as a student and teacher; the independent growth which she had made, formed a very different background for grief from that in Gerta's mind.

After a while Mrs. Marroner arose. She administered to herself a hot bath, a cold shower, a vigorous rubbing. "Now I can think," she said.

■ What is Mrs. Marroner going to think about?

## Passage 8

First she regretted the sentence of instant banishment. She went upstairs to see if it had been carried out. Poor Gerta! The tempest of her agony had worked itself out at last as in a child, and left her sleeping, the pillow wet, the lips still grieving, a big sob shuddering itself off now and then.

Mrs. Marroner stood and watched her, and as she watched she considered the helpless sweetness of the face; the defenseless, unformed character; the docility and habit of obedience which made her so attractive—and so easily a victim. Also she thought of the mighty force which had swept over her; of the great process now working itself out through her; of how pitiful and futile seemed any resistance she might have made.

She softly returned to her own room, made up a little fire, and sat by it, ignoring her feelings now, as she had before ignored her thoughts.

Here were two women and a man. One woman was a wife: loving, trusting, affectionate. One was a servant: loving, trusting, affectionate—a young girl, an exile, a dependent; grateful for any kindness; untrained, uneducated, childish. She ought, of course, to have resisted temptation; but Mrs. Marroner was wise enough to know how difficult temptation is to recognize when it comes in the guise of friendship and from a source one does not suspect.

Gerta might have done better in resisting the grocer's clerk; had, indeed, with Mrs. Marroner's advice, resisted several. But where respect was due, how could she criticize? Where obedience was due, how could she refuse—with ignorance to hold her blinded—until too late?

As the older, wiser woman forced herself to understand and extenuate the girl's misdeed and foresee her ruined future, a new feeling rose in her heart, strong, clear, and overmastering: a sense of measureless condemnation for the man who had done this thing. He knew. He understood. He could fully foresee and measure the consequences of his act. He appreciated to the full the innocence, the ignorance, the grateful affection, the habitual docility, of which he deliberately took advantage.

Mrs. Marroner rose to icy peaks of intellectual apprehension, from which her hours of frantic pain seemed far indeed removed. He had done this thing under the same roof with her—his wife. He had not frankly loved the younger woman, broken with his wife, made a new marriage. That would have been heart-break pure and simple. This was something else.

■ What does Mrs. Marroner mean by, "This was something else"?
■ Can you guess at how her thoughts are going to develop?

## Passage 9

That letter, that wretched, cold, carefully guarded, unsigned letter, that bill—far safer than a check—these did not speak of affection. Some men can love two women at one time. This was not love.

Mrs. Marroner's sense of pity and outrage for herself, the wife, now spread suddenly into a perception of pity and outrage for the girl. All that splendid, clean young beauty, the hope of a happy life, with marriage and motherhood, honorable independence, even—these were nothing to the man. For his own pleasure he had chosen to rob her of her life's best joys.

He would "take care of her," said the letter. How? In what capacity?

And then, sweeping over both her feelings for herself, the wife and Gerta, his victim, came a new flood, which literally lifted her to her feet. She rose and walked, her head held high.

"This is the sin of man against woman," she said. "The offense is against womanhood. Against motherhood. Against—the child."

She stopped.

The child. His child. That, too, he sacrificed and injured—doomed to degradation.

- What action do you think Mrs. Marroner is going to take now?
- What do you think is going to happen now, given that the story has moved on from its starting point?

## Passage 10

When Mr. Marroner reached home a few weeks later, following his letters too soon to expect an answer to either, he saw no wife upon the pier, though he had cabled, and found the house closed darkly. He let himself in with his latch-key, and stole softly upstairs, to surprise his wife.

No wife was there.

He rang the bell. No servant answered it.

He turned up light after light, searched the house from top to bottom; it was utterly empty. The kitchen wore a clean, bald, unsympathetic aspect. He left it and slowly mounted the stairs, completely dazed. The whole house was clean, in perfect order, wholly vacant.

One thing he felt perfectly sure of—she knew.

Yet was he sure? He must not assume too much. She might have been ill. She might have died. He started to his feet. No, they would have cabled him. He sat down again.

For any such change, if she had wanted him to know, she would have written. Perhaps she had, and he, returning so suddenly, had missed the letter. The thought was some comfort. It must be so. He turned to the telephone and again hesitated. If she had found out—if she had gone—utterly gone, without a word—should he announce it himself to friends and family?

He walked the floor; he searched everywhere for some letter, some word of explanation. Again and again he went to the telephone—and always stopped. He could not bear to ask: "Do you know where my wife is?"

The harmonious, beautiful rooms reminded him in a dumb, helpless way of her—like the remote smile on the face of the dead. He put out the lights, could not bear the darkness, turned them all on again.

It was a long night—

In the morning he went early to the office. In the accumulated mail was no letter from her. No one seemed to know of anything unusual. A friend asked after his wife—"Pretty glad to see you, I guess?" He answered evasively.

- What more do we learn about Mr. Marroner from this passage?
- How is he going to find out where his wife is?

## Passage 11

About eleven a man came to see him: John Hill, her lawyer. Her cousin, too. Mr. Marroner had never liked him. He liked him less now, for Mr. Hill merely handed him a letter, remarked, "I was requested to deliver this to you personally," and departed, looking like a person who is called on to kill something offensive.

"I have gone. I will care for Gerta. Good-bye. Marion."

That was all. There was no date, no address, no postmark, nothing but that.

In his anxiety and distress, he had fairly forgotten Gerta and all that. Her name aroused in him a sense of rage. She had come between him and his wife. She had taken his wife from him. That was the way he felt.

At first he said nothing, did nothing, lived alone in his house, taking meals where he chose. When people asked him about his wife, he said she was traveling—for her health. He would not have it in the newspapers. Then, as time passed, as no enlightenment came to him, he resolved not to bear it any longer, and employed detectives. They blamed him for not having put them on the track earlier, but set to work, urged to the utmost secrecy.

What to him had been so blank a wall of mystery seemed not to embarrass them in the least. They made careful enquiries as to her "past," found where she had studied, where taught, and on what lines; that she had some little money of her own, that her doctor was Josephine L. Bleet, M.D., and many other bits of information.

As a result of careful and prolonged work, they finally told him that she had resumed teaching under one of her old professors, lived quietly, and apparently kept boarders; giving him town, street, and number, as if it were a matter of no difficulty whatever.

He had returned in early spring. It was autumn before he found her.

■ What do Mr. Marroner's reactions to his wife's letter tell you about him?
■ What do you think he will do next and what will happen as a result?

## Passage 12

A quiet college town in the hills, a broad, shady street, a pleasant house standing in its own lawn, with trees and flowers about it. He had the address in his hand, and the number showed clear on the white gate. He walked up the straight gravel path and rang the bell. An elderly servant opened the door.

"Does Mrs. Marroner live here?"

"No, sir."

"This is number twenty-eight?"

"Yes, sir."

"Who does live here?"

"Miss Wheeling, sir."

Ah! Her maiden name. They told him, but he had forgotten.

He stepped inside. "I would like to see her," he said.

He was ushered into a still parlor, cool and sweet with the scent of flowers, the flowers she had always loved best. It almost brought tears to his eyes. All their years of happiness rose in his mind again—the exquisite beginnings; the days of eager longing before she was really his; the deep, still beauty of her love.

Surely she would forgive him—she must forgive him. He would humble himself; he would tell her of his honest remorse—his absolute determination to be a different man.

Through the wide doorway there came in to him two women. One like a tall madonna, bearing a baby in her arms.

Marion, calm, steady, definitely impersonal, nothing but a clear pallor to hint of inner stress.

Gerta, holding the child as a bulwark, with a new intelligence in her face, and her blue, adoring eyes fixed on her friend—not upon him.

He looked from one to the other dumbly.

And the woman who had been his wife asked quietly:

## The Ending

There is only one line of this story left. Can you predict what it might be?

■ Spend a few minutes in your groups deciding what Mrs. Marroner might say to her husband. (Note that it will be in question form.) When you have decided, you might find it interesting to compare your sentence with others in the class. They could be written on the chalkboard, and the class could decide on the ending it thinks most appropriate before reading the final sentence written by Gilman (see page 28).

You will probably want to spend a short time discussing the ending of "Turned" before undertaking the following activities, which ask you to compare the two short stories.

# Comparing "Turned" and "The Good Corn"

Briefly discuss the two stories with your partners or in your groups. Make notes on *any* similarities between them.

## The Characters

You have probably noted some general similarities between the three main characters of each story. It is worth making closer comparisons in order to develop your understanding of the way each character is constructed. The following list should help you compare the main characters of each story.

1. What are their names? How are they most often referred to in the story? Of what significance is their naming?

2. What are their ages? Of what significance are the ages of the characters?

3. What is the status of each character? What is their "position" in society? What is their position in relation to each other?

■ Draw a grid similar to the one below and, in your pair or group, write appropriate information in the Name/Age/Status section for each of the characters.

| Story | Information | Wife | Husband | Second Woman |
|---|---|---|---|---|
| "The Good Corn | Name<br>Age<br>Status | | | |
| | Presentation | | | |
| "Turned" | Name<br>Age<br>Status | | | |
| | Presentation | | | |

■ How do you believe each of the characters has been presented by the author? Do the details you are given encourage you to think sympathetically or unsympathetically about them? Using the words "sympathetic," "unsympathetic," and "neutral" (if you think the character isn't presented either way) fill in the Presentation sections of the grid.

■ Refer to the list you compiled earlier of adjectives used to describe Mr. and Mrs. Mortimer and Elsie. This is likely to be useful because the adjectives you listed should indicate your original response to the three main characters in H. E. Bates's story, and it may be interesting insofar as your views may have changed since reading "Turned."

## The Story Line

The story lines of "The Good Corn" and "Turned" have obvious similarities, too, but only up to a point.

■ In your pairs or groups, read through the events of the following story line and decide if what happens in each section also happens in "The Good Corn" and "Turned." Then decide whether it is (1) exactly the same, (2) nearly the same, or (3) different in each story.

| Story Line | 1 | 2 | 3 |
|---|---|---|---|
| 1. Husband and wife live alone. | | | |
| 2. They employ a young woman. | | | |
| 3. Young woman becomes pregnant. | | | |
| 4. Wife realizes husband is father of child. | | | |
| 5. Wife resolves to care for young woman and baby. | | | |
| 6. Wife forgives husband. | | | |
| 7. Birth of baby; young woman leaves. | | | |
| 8. Husband and wife together with baby. | | | |

When you have finished, look back at your comparison of the story lines and, in your groups, consider the following questions:

■ How similar are the two stories?
■ At what stage do the events become different? Construct a separate story line for "Turned" from this point on.
■ Why do you think the writers chose to have their characters make different decisions and take different actions at this point?

## Why Did She Leave?

One major difference between the two stories is that Mrs. Marroner doesn't forgive her husband. Instead she leaves, taking the "other woman" with her.

■ In your pairs or groups, choose three or four of the following statements which you think *best* sum up Mrs. Marroner's reasons for leaving her husband. Be prepared to support your decisions.

Mrs. Marroner leaves her husband because she:

1. is hurt and upset.
2. wants to punish him for his infidelity.
3. no longer loves him.
4. no longer respects him.
5. is hard and unforgiving.
6. feels a responsibility to the child.
7. feels he has taken unfair advantage of Gerta.
8. believes he has behaved dishonorably.
9. wants to teach him a lesson.

10. feels he has betrayed their love.
11. feels she has a responsibility to Gerta.
12. is highly moral.

# Role Play

A good way to get to know a story, and to explore its construction and the ideas that seem to be at work in it, is to try to get "inside" the story and see things through the eyes of the characters in it. One way of doing this is by talking in role—that is, as if you were a character in the story.

■ In your groups, try performing the following role play involving Mrs. Marroner.

Here is one possible situation: Mr. Marroner contests the separation between himself and his wife and sends an intermediary to speak to Mrs. Marroner. The intermediary's job is to find out the reasons why Mrs. Marroner has behaved as she has, what her motives and feelings are, and whether she would contemplate a reconciliation with her husband.

■ Your group should divide into pairs—one pair to act as the intermediary, the other to take the part of Mrs. Marroner. (Doing this part of the activity in pairs gives you the opportunity to talk about and try out your ideas before performing in role.)

■ The students acting as intermediary need to think of the questions they will ask Mrs. Marroner to discover her motives and her rationale for acting as she does. The intermediary could start by asking Mrs. Marroner to identify herself and give some details of her background. Then move on to questions about her relationship with her husband, the discovery of the pregnancy, her husband's paternity, her own feelings about these things, and her reasons for the course of action she takes.

■ The students taking the part of Mrs. Marroner should begin to prepare themselves for the kind of questions the intermediary will ask by revising what they know about her from their reading of "Turned." (Remember that you must answer in role.)

■ You may wish, after a group rehearsal, to choose one Mrs. Marroner and one intermediary to present your group's role play to a wider audience. However, there is nothing to stop you from performing your role play in pairs as long as you work out an arrangement for speaking.

■ You may think of some other possible scenarios to present as role plays as alternatives, or additions, to this one.

## After the Inquiry

■ In a whole class discussion, share your opinions of Mrs. Marroner's behavior and her reasons for acting as she did.

■ Comment on how easy or difficult you thought the text made it to act in role. For example, how much information is presented for the reader to construct a picture of Mrs. Marroner's reasons for leaving her husband and looking after Gerta? How visible are the writer's assumptions about the nature of "fair" behavior between women and men?

## For Discussion

As you have discovered, the characters and the story lines of "The Good Corn" and "Turned" are similar in many ways. And yet they are very different stories that ask to be read in very different ways.

A major difference between the two stories is the different way in which the two wives are presented as reacting to their husbands' infidelity. The husbands could be said to act in similar ways, yet Mrs. Mortimer is forgiving and "understanding" while Mrs. Marroner leaves home with Gerta.

■ Spend some time discussing the following questions, recording your main points in note form.

1. What effect does Mrs. Marroner's departure with Gerta have on how her husband's actions are seen by the reader, compared with how the presentation of the apparently similar actions of Joe Mortimer in "The Good Corn" asks to be read?

2. Why do you think the writers of these stories have chosen to present characters in similar situations in quite different ways?

3. What effect does Mrs. Mortimer's forgiveness of her husband, Joe, have on how the character Elsie is seen by the reader, compared with how Gerta is seen?

4. Having read "Turned," do you think you now might read "The Good Corn" differently? If so, *how* would your reading now differ from your first reading?

# A Touch of Class?

"Turned" is a story which has the effect of calling into question issues related to gender. Does it have the same effect when dealing with matters related to social class? This is a similar kind of activity to the earlier role play, but it takes the form of a series of questions put to Mrs. Marroner by an unsympathetic interrogator. The questions asked by the interrogator are based on the following descriptions of Gerta in "Turned":

- "childish"
- "ignorant"
- "Little Gerta"
- "untutored"
- "unusually teachable"
- "her dullness"
- "meek young goddess"

- "visible limitations"
- "willing"
- "docile"
- "foolish"
- "ignorant child"
- "her eager obedience"
- "plastic"

- Read the passage below, completing Mrs. Marroner's replies in role, and asking any other questions you think relevant.

Interrogator: (smiling) You say, Mrs. Marroner, that you and your husband cared for Gerta?

Mrs. Marroner: (coolly) I don't wish to answer for Mr. Marroner. I was most concerned about her welfare.

Interrogator: You were fond of her even?

Mrs. Marroner: Yes.

Interrogator: You don't have children of your own, Mrs. Marroner, do you?

Mrs. Marroner: (suppressing anger at the intrusion) No.

Interrogator: So Gerta was almost a substitute daughter to you?

Mrs. Marroner: (distantly) In some ways. I suppose so.

Interrogator: Which would explain why you referred to her on various occasions as a "big child," "child-like," "naïve," and so on?

Mrs. Marroner: . . .

Interrogator: You spoke too on occasion of trying to "improve" her. Why did you think she needed "improvement"?

Mrs. Marroner: . . .

Interrogator: And why did you refer to Gerta as "limited" and even "ignorant"?

Mrs. Marroner: . . .

Interrogator: (openly sarcastic) But you cared for her anyway, Mrs. Marroner, this child-like, limited, ignorant, foolish young woman in need of improvement?

Mrs. Marroner: . . .

Interrogator: And yet Gerta's room in your house is described as an "uncarpeted, thin-curtained, poorly-furnished chamber on the top floor" in which she had to sleep on a "narrow, hard bed." How do you account for this?

Mrs. Marroner: . . .

## Gaps in the text?

This activity may reveal some *gaps* in "Turned." For example, you may have found it hard to answer in role as Mrs. Marroner about Gerta's room, because her writer hasn't given her anything to say, or at least—to modern readers—anything very acceptable to say.

Charlotte Perkins Gilman presents Gerta's poorly furnished room without comment because she takes it for granted that a woman of Gerta's class—a servant—would have an accommodation of this standard. You could ask yourself why the description (at the beginning of passage two) is there at all.

## For Discussion

1. What other assumptions about social class are made in this story?
2. Mr. Marroner's "story" is not told in "Turned." Is this gap the same kind of gap as the one suggested above? For example, do you think that Charlotte Perkins Gilman was unaware of the kind of defense the character of Mr. Marroner could have put forward, or does it seem a conscious decision on her part not to present it?

# For Writing

The two stories you have read explore the relationships between one man and two women. Traditionally, in stories which evolve around this triangular grouping of characters, one of the women is often presented in an unsympathetic manner. Charlotte Perkins Gilman's story "Turned" is unusual in that it clearly deflects the reader's sympathy away from the man and provides an unusual solution to the problem faced by the two women. This is one example of writing "against the grain" or of creating a story that is quite plausible even though it does not offer the expected solution.

■ Try writing your own story using only three characters—two women and one man—*or* you could vary the situation by using two men and one woman. Aim to create a story that does not fit the pattern of "normal expectations."

1. Begin your story by deciding which two characters will be introduced first; will it be a traditional man/woman situation or will there be two women friends or two male friends? Introduce your characters by telling the reader who they are, where they live, and what they do. You could also include some particulars about their background if these are important for the development of your story.

2. Introduce some incident that causes disharmony between the pair while at the same time drawing the third character into the action.

3. Concentrate on developing the conflict between the characters.

4. Resolve the situation by producing some believable solution to the problem. You should try to think of something that would be unusual. Alternatively, you could end on an ambiguous note.

■ Use one of the following sentences from the story (Column A) as the first line of your own story. Tell it from the point of view of the character in Column B.

| Column A | Column B |
| --- | --- |
| Her brown eyes travelled over the fields as if she were looking for something she had lost there. (p. 5) | Elsie |
| "Go to your room and pack," said Mrs. Marroner. (p. 17) | Gerta |
| "Be good to your mistress, Gerta. . . . I leave her to you to take care of. I shall be back in a month at latest." (p. 14) | Mr. Marroner |
| "Don't say that. Don't talk like that. . . . You're not well. You're not yourself. I'm going to get the doctor to look at you." (p. 3) | Joe Mortimer |

# The Last Line of "Turned"

"What have you to say to us?"

# 2 Intentions

- Are the meanings readers make always what writers intend?
- Can stories have "messages" unintended by the writer?
- What are "gaps" or "silences" in a story?
- Can the way a story is read change over time?
- Do readers distort a story by reading it in a way that it doesn't ask?

## "What Katie Did" and "The Great Leapfrog Contest"

"What Katie Did" by Sid Chaplin and "The Great Leapfrog Contest" by William Saroyan are both about adventurous, non-conforming young women. Katie and Rosie are presented as strong, even rebellious, protagonists who challenge the expectations the society of their day has of how young women should behave. In this chapter, the reading of both stories is interrupted by removing short sections from them and by asking you to predict the choices the writers might have made in the presentation of their characters. The purpose of these interruptions (which are marked by asterisks) is to make it easier for you to question and explore the decisions made by the writers.

## "What Katie Did"

This story is by the English writer Sid Chaplin, who was brought up in a mining family in the Northeast of England. The title alludes to the popular novel *What Katy Did* by the American writer Susan Coolidge; first published in 1873, Coolidge's book portrays Katy Carr, who "tore her dress every day, hated sewing, and didn't care a button about being called good."

## What Katie Did _____

*Sid Chaplin*

Twice a week I go to see Aunt Katie. It is not out of any sense of duty. Nor do I go to collect rent-money or insurance or anything like that. It is because I am in love with her.

It is because she is small and lively; it is because she is pretty still; it is because she laughs one minute and is serious the next; it is because she can make you laugh too; it is because she can tell the tale.

\* All her tales are about the green valley in which we live. She knows every nook and cranny of it. She knows all the notable figures. She knows more about them than they know themselves. Only one tale is about any other place than this valley with its pits and pit-people, its crazy rows of houses and whitewashed pigeon-crees.[1] It is about the time when she ran away from home.

She had just left school and had started work. Making bricks was her job. She stamped out the wet clay into bricks; they went into a beehive oven to be baked and that was the last she saw of them. It was wet clay every day that God sent. She worked nine and a half hours with it, and when she went home at night there was clay in her hair, clay on her hands and behind her finger-nails; and her clogs dragged, heavy with clay. She hated it. But when she got home her work was not finished. There were meals to be got ready for her Da and her brothers coming in from the pit; five pairs of heavy pit-boots to clean and wet pit-clothes to dry for the next shift.

She was the only daughter left at home. The other three had got married. They got married to get away from cleaning pit-boots. But Katie was original. One day she said to her Ma, "Ah'm not going to clean any more pit-boots. They can clean their own." Ma was flabbergasted.

Then she recovered her senses. "You get them boots cleaned," she said, "or you'll get a good tannin' where it hurts most."

But Katie was determined. She wouldn't clean those boots. So she got a good tanning. And when her Da got to know, he gave her a clout that sent her spinning across the kitchen. And the lads gave her no peace at all.

So she ran away. She went to the next county to an Aunt of hers who had married a farmer. Long before, Katie had spent a joyous holiday with this Aunt, and she remembered the rolling moors and mighty meals they had, and no pit-boots to clean.

"My sangs," said her aunt, "whatever in God's creation brings you here, our little Katie?"

"Pit-boots," said Katie. Her aunt stared at her, then smiled, then laughed till the tears trickled down her red cheeks. Then she asked no more but got high tea ready. This was home-fed ham and home-made bread and great mugs of creamy tea, and if ever you've had a meal better than this you're lucky.

Then she sent Katie off to see the hens while she wrote a letter to my Grandmother. What she put in that letter nobody ever got to know, but the outcome was that Katie had to stay for a long holiday.

It was a grand holiday. Katie and her cousins roamed up and down the dale, went for picnics, and in between fed the hens and the pigs. And feeding hens and pigs is an exciting adventure after you've been feeding a brick oven.

---

1. *Cree*, a dialect word in northern England, refers to a small hut or pen.

Did she like it? She took to it like a duck takes to water. She never wanted to see Deepdown again. But she knew a holiday must end some day. She knew that the day would come when she'd have to go back to brickmaking and the cleaning of pit-boots. So she decided to get a job. She looked every day at the advertisements in the *Dale Advertiser* and one day she saw what she wanted. She wrote a letter in her best handwriting, posted it, then got up early every morning to meet the postman. She knew that if her Aunt saw a letter there would be questions, that's why she went out on the sly to meet the postman.

And one day she got a reply saying that she was to go for an interview. She secretly crept away to the great house, walked up the winding drive to the front door. There she pulled a shining chain and listened to a bell clanging.

The door opened and a magnificent person, who seemed seven foot high, with terrible eyes and a hooked nose, was looking down upon her, as if some species of worm was writhing upon the door-step. He was dressed in old-fashioned clothes, she said.

He summed her up in a split second.

"What can I do for you my good girl?" he said.

"Please," she said, "Ah've come about the job."

He made a shocked motion of the hands. "The servants' entrance is at the rear," he said.

My Aunt Katie has a temper as well. "Ah'm not a servant yet," she said.

"The servants' entrance is at the rear my good girl," he replied distantly, and closed the door in her face.

So she went to the back of the house. She passed a row of kennels in which were dogs that barked at her. There were stables and a courtyard with a lad brushing down a horse. It was a good horse, Katie knew, because how many times had she not listened to her Da debating about horse-flesh? "Hey," she shouted to the lad, "that's a good horse you've got there!" The lad opened his mouth to say something cheeky in answer, then his eyes widened at something he saw over Katie's shoulder and he touched his cap. She turned and saw a shabbily-dressed man with a weather beaten face. His mouth was wrinkled in a smile, so she smiled too. "What makes you think she's a good horse?" he said. "Neck, legs and head," said Katie, and proceeded to amplify. The man listened with respect. "Where'd you learn all this?" he asked. "Off my Da," she replied, "he likes a bet and he talks a lot about horses. And he cuts pictures of them out of the paper and hangs them in his pigeon-cree." "Pigeon fancier, too, eh?" said the man.

"Pigeon fancier!" she cried. "He's won more races with his birds than you have hairs on your head." He pulled off his tweed cap with a grin, and she saw that he was almost bald. "Well," she said defensively, "he's won more races than you *used* to have hairs on your head."

"Indeed," said the man, "but what may your business be here today, my small judge of horseflesh and feathers?"

"Oh," she said, "the swanks that live in the big house there want a maid, so Ah'm applying for the job." He smiled and passed her.

He walked up to the mare and stroked her head. "How's the fetlock, Harry?" he asked. "Doing fine, Sir Robert," He turned back to Katie, whose mouth had widened to a beautiful "O" at the "Sir." "You'd better hurry up and see the swanks before they give someone else the job," he said.

At the back door she was received by the magnificent gentleman with the old-fashioned clothes, but this time minus his coat. "So you found your way, eh?" he said, and pulled on his coat again. "Follow me."

They went through winding corridors and through a vast hall, then up a winding staircase. He stopped outside a door and bent down to whisper in her ear, "Stay here, my good girl, till I return for you." He knocked carefully, entered, then returned. "Her ladyship will see you." he said. He opened the door and she passed through.

The room was gorgeous: everything rose pink: and in the centre a desk at which a lady was writing. It was the Great Hostess. The great lady asked her a few questions, smiled at her, then rang the bell. The butler returned. "You may take the girl to Mrs. Ramshaw," she said.

Mrs. Ramshaw was the housekeeper. She was tall and never smiled. Her long black dress went to her ankles. Her eyes went through Katie's body. Katie felt that nothing could be hidden from this woman. And she was right. Mrs. Ramshaw was the real mistress of the house, the unseen, noiseless engine that kept the great house alive. In five minutes all was settled. She was to commence tomorrow. She was to live in. She would be kept, uniforms provided, and she would be paid fifteen pounds a year. Then she was dismissed, to walk back to the farm in a daze, there to be admired, admonished, and told that Sir Robert was her master.

"I don't know what your Ma will say," said her Aunt. Another letter was written.

Life at the big house was ups and downs. When Katie worked for Mrs. Ramshaw it was all downs. Mrs. Ramshaw was a slave-driver.

But sometimes she assisted the Head Butler, and that was interesting and exciting. Mr. Sangster was round-shouldered with a curiously flat face that was always placid. He had served in great houses all his life and could reel off the names of the aristocracy as a miner will recite the names of famous footballers. And, as a miner can trace the pedigree of his whippet, so could he track down the forebears of Lords and Ladies. And he knew their secrets as well as he knew the dark places of their halls. Mention some Duke and he would go into a rapturous trance, mumbling the complicated story of relations and inter-relations. And pride! A miner may rise to the Cabinet; a mill-lad may become a millionaire; but nothing compared to his rise from boot-boy to head butler, Lord of the Pantry and High Priest of the Silver!

Katie took him in hand. One day they went up to Leeds to see a football match. Mr. Sangster escaped from his pantry for one wild hour and yelled with the crowd. But he never went to Leeds again. He was slightly ashamed of himself and implored Katie not to tell.

She didn't greatly care for the life. Only one thing kept her working: the memory of clay and pit-boots. She loved the good food and the splendour; but her soul rebelled against servility, and if the servants had one thing in common it was this.

Madam floated through the rooms like a vision; Sir Robert came in for his meals, then slouched back to his horses or the kennels. Then Madam began to get up late; the whisper went round the servant's hall that an heir was expected.

Katie was in the wine-cellar one day when Sir Robert wandered down to select some bottles to be sent to a friend. The wine-cellar was his department. "Hello, lassie," he said. "How d'you like working for the swanks, now?"

"Oh, it's not so bad," said Katie.

"Well," he said, "I'm pleased to hear that."

"And Ah was pleased to hear about the baby coming," said Katie. "I hope it's a lovely little boy."

"Good Lord!" he cried. "How on earth did you get to know?"

Now Katie had heard first about it from Cook, but she didn't want to split. "Oh, I've got eyes," she said carelessly, remembering a favorite phrase of her mother.

"Well, I'll be damned," he said. "How old are you?" "Sixteen and a half, sir." He raised his eyebrows. "Here's half-a-crown, and keep your mouth shut." She refused the half-crown. "I can keep a secret," she said, "but I don't want paying for it, sir." "Don't be such a little fool, lassy," he said. "You take it and buy some chocs."

So she took it and went up the flight of steps. When she got to the door she turned round and looked down. "Well?" he said. She smiled. "Ah hope it's a boy." He stared back for a moment, then smiled back. It takes a good man to stand up to Auntie Katie's smile. "So do I," he said.


It was the dinner party that finished Katie's career. She might have been housekeeper there now, if it hadn't been for that dinner party.

Madam decided to have this dinner party before her temporary retirement. It was to be a great affair, designed to keep her reputation as a great hostess alive during her long absence. There was a flurry of excitement and preparation; long conferences with Mrs. Ramshaw and Mr. Sangster. The silver was polished until it was like glass, then polished again until every piece seemed a rare, unreal thing. Then, three days before the great event, half the staff went down with flu. In a moment of madness it was arranged that Katie should help serve. Madness, because he or she who serves the meals of the aristocracy must be a silent efficient machine.

The fatal evening arrived, and with it the guests. Generals and admirals came; there was a lord and his lady; and last, but not least, a notable bishop, whose love of good food and wine exceeded his love for matters spiritual.

The table was a splendid sight, said my Aunt Katie, all a glitter with silver and the flame of splendid candles. After all those years she still remembered the food and wine, though she confessed she might have them in the wrong order.

There was hors-d'oeuvre first, then turtle soup. There was a noble saddle of mutton or, for those who did not care for this solid fare, there was duck. There was a luscious sweet of rich strawberry cream, or, if this palled, the more enlivening brandy-snap. For savoury there were devils on horseback, and these delightful devils the bishop devoured with amazing speed. Then came dessert with an abundance of almonds, peaches, nectarines and grapes, with fondants and Turkish Delight.

And the wines? There was a rare sherry; Liebfraumilch poured from slender, tapered bottles into balloon glasses; and an ancient Burgundy, rounded off with a medley of matured liqueurs. Oh, and there was coffee, and if you are amazed that such splendid people in the midst of such richness should bother with coffee, I will tell you that Cook was a past-mistress in the rare art of making coffee; so it was that Madam was far-famed for her delightful coffee.

The food was perfect, the wines superb, and all might have gone well had it not been that Katie was serving. The first rift occurred during the serving of the main course, when, confronted with a choice of two sauces, the undecided Bishop was advised that the one was better than the other. With true Christian humility, the Bishop accepted the advice, the nearer guests stared in absolute astonishment, Madam went crimson, Mr. Sangster pale. Sir Robert smiled.

Hastily reprimanded behind the dining-room doors, Katie was sent back to do better. This she did. During dessert, the conversation turned to investments. An admiral confessed that he was considering an investment with a mining concern. Katie was at once all afire with interest and excitement, she knew the firm's name all too well. The bishop, having disposed of a mouthful of nectarine, gave his advice. "Keep clear of these mining concerns, my dear Edward," he said, "a most uncertain industry; and I hear that that one is having a rather difficult time."

"Oh no!" cried Katie, "they're a very big firm, and they've got the best pits in the country. I should know. My Da and all my brothers work for them."

There was a deep silence, broken only by the eventual coughing of Sir Robert, a choking cough which in some measure, succeeded in distracting attention from the awful spectacle of a talking menial.

But the damage was done. Puzzled glances were cast at the once great hostess, and uncertain whisperings testified to a general astonishment. For the first time the great lady looked forward with some relief to her confinement; this at least Katie did.

But the worst was yet to come. Dessert was finished, the ladies departed for coffee, leaving the admirals and all in unrestrained freedom. It was unfortunate that the ladies should choose a most controversial subject and one which raised Katie's ire. Her short-comings before had been a mixture of naivety and a certain chumminess, which comes easily to those born and bred in pit villages, but the new subject aroused her temper and led to the final scene of that unusual evening.

Encouraged by the retreat of the great lady to some private place where she could regain her composure, the female guests had embarked on a general discussion of the events of the evening and the amazing cheek of the little slavey. This had led to the subject of the mining community, since the country was at the time being held to ransom by a nation-wide strike of these dissatisfied plutocrats. The conversation touched upon the fat wage packets earned: Katie remained silent. There were fleeting references to miner's wives who flaunted their fur coats; and Katie had a vision of her hard-working mother, tied to an eternal cycle of scrubbing, washing and cooking, and bit her bottom lip until a tiny trickle of crimson stained her pointed chin. The conversation touched upon luxury in which the miner's whippet was kept—rich steaks and chops and diced liver, while the children went barefooted. But when one young thing spoke with contempt of the gambling habits of the mining people, all restraint went by the wind.

"Cats," Katie cried, "sneaking, overfed, slinking cats, the lot of you. Why, the meal you've just eaten would keep my family in luxury for a year. And as for you," she cried, pointing at the startled debutante, whose foolish mouth now hung askew at this attack, "the fruit you ate for dessert would pay all my Dad's bets for a twelve month."

They sat petrified like images, the fat and the thin, with their dazzling gowns and flashing jewellery, with their rigid faces; twisted lips forming distorted "O's."

Katie surveyed them with contempt. "Well," she concluded, "if your brains were as big as your mouths you'd be really brilliant people." And she set down the tray with such a clatter that it shook its fragile polished legs. And then she was gone.

The next day she packed. But first she said goodbye to Mr. Sangster and the stable boy and Cook. Mr. Sangster was sorry, yet pleased. No one could fail to love Katie, least of all Mr. Sangster; but she had upset his world; and she knew about the football match; she was the one person in the world who had seen Mr. Sangster shout, "Goal!" I think the stable-boy was in love with Katie; anyway, he promised to write, so he must have been. Cook was a genius in her own way, an aristocrat. She was so good a cook that she could hold her own anywhere. She was not afraid of Mrs. Ramshaw, she had a great contempt for almost everyone at the great house. She was a free-born democrat who shook with laughter when Katie told her what she had done and said.

Then Katie went to the wine-cellar and got half-a-dozen bottles of Chianti to take home for her Dad. She put them in her bag underneath her clothes and was just pressing the clasp down to lock it when there came a knock at the door. "Come in," she said. Sir Robert wandered in. "Thought I'd drop in to say goodbye," he said. "Goodbye," said Katie. "Not so fast as that," he said with a smile. "Can I help you to pack?" So she sat down on the bag. "I'm finished packing," she said. "Oh, no," he answered, and pulled a box of cigars out of his pocket. "Find room for these," he said, "Give them to your Dad, with my regards."

She took the box. He walked to the window and looked out, then came over to the bed and held out his hand. "Well, thanks for last night. I was with you all the time. It was great. Goodbye." She had to stand up then and shake hands.

Then he said, "I'll have to go now." He went to the door, opened it, then turned again. "Have a bottle of that Chianti with your Dad when you get home. It's good stuff. Keep it for special occasions, and drink it slowly. And don't forget to toast your old friend."

And when they opened the first bottle in the pigeon-cree, with the pictures of racers pinned up all around them, with the pigeons cooing and fluttering and stepping delicately in the loft, you can bet your boots my Aunt Katie didn't forget.

## What Will Katie Do?

Having read "What Katie Did," and knowing Katie's spirit, her sense of independence (that both gained and lost her the job in the grand house), her liking for the good life, and her loyalty to her own people, what sort of future would you predict for her after she has returned to her family?

▪ In your groups, talk about what you think Katie could go on to do. Make a list of three or four possibilities that you consider likely, given what you know about Katie and the world in which she lives.

## What Katie Does

The following paragraph was deleted from near the beginning of the story. It describes what Katie actually is doing as an adult:

She will be dusting, or baking, or cooking a dinner or maybe she will be scrubbing the kitchen floor. All will go by the board. The duster will drop from her hand, the bread will rise and billow over the tins, the dinner will spoil and the scrubbing brush will drop back into the pail until the tale is told.

What does it imply that Katie did after she returned to her family?

## The Writer's Intentions

Discuss the following statements and say which best describe the writer's intentions and his attitude to Katie's early rebellion. The writer:

1. wants to show that girls like Katie do eventually settle down and become good housewives.

2. wants to show there was no escape from hard work for girls like Katie.

3. shows how sad it was that Katie had to go back to the cleaning and cooking that she used to hate.

4. admires Katie's independence and her youthful rebelliousness, but accepts the reality that Katie didn't have many choices in life.

5. presents Katie's early rebellion, both at home and in the great house, as symbolic of wider protest against class and gender discrimination.

6. is simply "telling the tale"; he hasn't really thought about the meaning or significance of Katie's early actions.

7. intends the reader to feel angry at the injustice in Katie's life.

8. approves of Katie running away from home and her first job, and her rebelliousness at the great house, but sees her later life when she is again doing housework as a natural and not unhappy one for a woman.

# "The Great Leapfrog Contest"

The next story was written by the American writer William Saroyan. Again, some text has been removed in order to let you predict the choices the writer might have made in presenting the characters. The story is followed by questions that will help you consider the possibilities, as well as a section inviting you to compare the two stories through discussion and activities.

## The Great Leapfrog Contest _____

*William Saroyan*

Rosie Mahoney was a tough little Irish kid whose folks had moved into the Russian-Italian-and-Greek neighborhood of my home town, across the Southern Pacific tracks, around G Street.

She wore a turtle-neck sweater, usually red. Her father was a bricklayer named Cull and a heavy drinker. Her mother's name was Mary. Mary Mahoney used to go to the Greek Orthodox Catholic Church on Kearny Boulevard every Sunday, because there was no Irish Church to go to anywhere in the neighborhood. The family seemed to be a happy one.

Rosie's three brothers had all grown up and gone to sea. Her two sisters had married. Rosie was the last of the clan. She had entered the world when her father had been close to sixty and her mother in her early fifties. For all that, she was hardly the studious or scholarly type.

Rosie had little use for girls, and as far as possible avoided them. She had less use for boys, but found it undesirable to avoid them. That is to say, she made it a point to take part in everything the boys did. She was always on hand, and always the first to take up any daring or crazy idea. Everybody felt awkward about her continuous presence but it was no use trying to chase her away, because that meant a fight in which she asked no quarter, and gave none.

If she didn't whip every boy she fought, every fight was at least an honest draw, with a slight edge in Rosie's favor. She didn't fight girl-style, or cry if hurt. She fought the regular style and took advantage of every opening. It was very humiliating to be hurt by Rosie, so after a while any boy who thought of trying to chase her away, decided not to.

It was no use. She just wouldn't go. She didn't seem to like any of the boys especially, but she liked being in on any mischief they might have in mind, and she wanted to play on any teams they organized. She was an excellent baseball player, being as good as anybody else in the neighborhood at any position, and for her age an expert pitcher. She had a wicked wing, too, and could throw a ball in from left field so that when it hit the catcher's mitt it made a nice sound.

She was extraordinarily swift on her feet and played a beautiful game of tin-can hockey.

At pee-wee, she seemed to have the most disgusting luck in the world.

At the game we invented and used to call *Horse* she was as good at *horse* as at *rider*, and she insisted on following the rules of the game. She insisted on being horse when it was her turn to be horse. This always embarrassed her partner, whoever he happened to be, because it didn't seem right for a boy to be getting up on the back of a girl.

She was an excellent football player too.

As a matter of fact, she was just naturally the equal of any boy in the neighborhood, and much the superior of many of them. Especially after she had lived in the neighborhood three years. It took her that long to make everybody understand that she had come to stay and that she was *going* to stay.

She did, too: even after the arrival of a boy name Rex Folger, who was from somewhere in the south of Texas. This boy Rex was a natural-born leader. Two months after his arrival in the neighborhood, it was understood by everyone that if Rex wasn't the leader of the gang, he was very nearly the leader. He had fought and licked every boy in the neighborhood who at one time or another had fancied himself leader. And he had done so without any noticeable ill-feeling, pride or ambition.

As a matter of fact, no-one could possibly have been more good-natured than Rex. Everybody resented him, just the same.

One winter, the whole neighborhood took to playing a game that had become popular on the other side of the tracks, in another slum neighborhood of the town: *Leapfrog.* The idea was for as many boys as cared to participate, to bend down and be leaped over by every other boy in the game, and then himself to get up and begin leaping over all the other boys, and then bend down again until all the boys had leaped over him again, and keep this up until all the other players had become exhausted. This didn't happen, sometimes, until the last two players had traveled a distance of three or four miles while the other players walked along, watching and making bets.

Rosie, of course, was always in on the game. She was always one of the last to drop out, too. And she was the only person in the neighborhood Rex Folger hadn't fought and beaten.

He felt that that was much too humiliating even to think about. But inasmuch as she seemed to be a member of the gang, he felt that in some way or another he ought to prove his superiority.

One summer day during vacation, an argument between Rex and Rosie developed and Rosie pulled off her turtle-neck sweater and challenged him to a fight. Rex told Rosie he wasn't in the habit of hitting women—where he came from that amounted to boxing your mother. On the other hand, he said, if Rosie cared to compete with him in any other sport, he would be glad to oblige her. Rex was a very calm and courteous conversationalist. He had poise. It was unconscious of course, but he had it just the same. He was just naturally a man who couldn't be hurried, flustered, or excited.

So Rex and Rosie fought it out in this game Leapfrog. They got to leaping over one another, quickly, too, until the first thing we knew the whole gang of us was out on the State Highway going south towards Fowler. It was a very hot day. Rosie and Rex were in great shape, and it looked like none was tougher than the other and more stubborn. They talked a good deal, especially Rosie, who insisted that she would have to fall down unconscious before she'd give up to a guy like Rex.

He said he was sorry his opponent was a girl. It grieved him deeply to have to make a girl exert herself to the point of death, but it was just too bad. He had to, so he had to. They leaped and squatted, leaped and squatted, and we got out to Sam Day's vineyard. That was half-way to Fowler. It didn't seem like either Rosie or Rex were ever going to get tired. They hadn't even begun to show signs of growing tired, although each of them was sweating a great deal.

Naturally, we were sure Rex would win the contest. But that was because we hadn't taken into account the fact that he was a simple person, whereas Rosie was crafty and shrewd. Rosie knew how to figure angles. She had discovered how to jump over Rex Folger in a way that weakened him. And after a while, about three miles out of Fowler, we noticed that she was coming down on Rex's *neck*, instead of on his back. Naturally, this was hurting him and making the blood rush to his head. Rosie herself squatted in such a way that it was impossible, almost, for Rex to get any-where near her neck with his hands.

Before long, we noticed that Rex was weakening. His head was getting closer and closer to the ground. About half a mile out of Fowler, we heard Rex's head bumping the ground every time Rosie leaped over him. They were good loud bumps that we knew were painful, but Rex wasn't complaining. He was too proud to complain.

Rosie, on the other hand, knew she had her man, and she was giving him all she had. She was bumping his head on the ground as solidly as she could, because she knew she didn't have much more fight in her, and if she didn't lay him out cold, in the hot sun, in the next ten minutes or so, she would fall down exhausted herself, and lose the contest.

Suddenly Rosie bumped Rex's head a real powerful one. He got up very dazed and very angry. It was the first time we had ever seen him fuming. By God, the girl was taking advantage of him if he wasn't mistaken, and he didn't like it. Rosie was squatted in front of him. He came up groggy and paused a moment. Then he gave Rosie a very effective kick that sent her sprawling, Rosie jumped up and smacked Rex in the mouth. The gang jumped in and tried to establish order.

It was agreed that the Leapfrog contest must not change into a fight. Not any more. Not with Fowler only five or ten minutes away. The gang ruled further that Rex had no right to kick Rosie and that in smacking him in the mouth Rosie had squared the matter, and the contest was to continue.

Rosie was very tired and sore; and so was Rex. They began leaping and squatting again: and again we saw Rosie coming down on Rex's neck so that his head was bumping the ground.

It looked pretty bad for the boy from Texas. We couldn't understand how he could take so much punishment. We all felt that Rex was getting what he had coming to him, but at the same time everybody seemed to feel badly about Rosie, a girl, doing the job instead of one of us. Of course, that was where we were wrong. Nobody but Rosie could have figured out that smart way of humiliating a very powerful and superior boy.*

Less than a hundred yards from the heart of Fowler, Rosie, with great and admirable artistry, finished the job.

That was where the dirt of the highway siding ended and the paved main street of Fowler began. This street was paved with cement, not asphalt. Asphalt, in that heat, would have been too soft to serve, but cement had exactly the right degree of brittleness. I think Rex when he squatted over the hard cement, knew the game was up. But he was brave to the end. He squatted over the hard cement and waited for the worst. Behind him, Rosie Mahoney prepared to make the supreme effort. In this next leap, she intended to give her all, which she did.

She came down on Rex Folger's neck like a ton of bricks. His head banged against the hard cement, his body straightened out, and his arms and legs twitched.

He was out like a light.

Six paces in front of him, Rosie Mahoney squatted and waited. Jim Telesco counted twenty, which was the time allowed for each leap. Rex didn't get up during the count.

The contest was over. The winner of the contest was Rosie Mahoney.

Rex didn't get up by himself at all. He just stayed where he was until a half-dozen of us lifted him and carried him to a horse-trough, where we splashed water on his face.

Rex was a confused young man all the way back. He was also a deeply humiliated one. He couldn't understand anything about anything. He just looked dazed and speechless. Every now and then we imagined he wanted to talk, and I guess he did, but after we'd all gotten ready to hear what he had to say, he couldn't speak. He made a gesture so tragic that tears came to the eyes of eleven members of the gang.

Rosie Mahoney, on the other hand, talked all the way home. She said everything.**

# What Will Rosie Do?

A few sentences were deleted from the story. They describe what happened to Rosie a few months later and then five years later.

■ Below are two sets of statements that suggest some possibilities. Choose one from each set that comes closest to what you think might have happened to Rosie. You may be able to make a link between your two choices.

A few months later, Rosie:

1. became the first girl to lead the gang.

2. had a bad accident that kept her at home for a long time.

3. decided to take her school work seriously and became a model student.

4. left the gang and wasn't seen around much.

5. calmed down a lot and made friends with Rex.

6. became the school's star player at basketball.

Five years later, Rosie:

1. published her first book of short stories.

2. was a member of the American women's basketball team.

3. joined the army.

4. married a wealthy and influential young man.

5. won the local beauty contest.

6. moved away from the area and was never heard of again.

These are the passages about Rosie that were deleted from your first reading of "The Great Leapfrog Contest."

* It was probably the woman in her, which, less than five years later, came out to such an extent that she became one of the most beautiful girls in town, gave up tomboy activities and married one of the wealthiest young men in Kings County, a college man named, if memory serves, Wallace Hadington Finlay VI.

** That winter Rosie Mahoney stopped hanging around with the gang too. She had a flair for making an exit at the right time.

■ In your groups, consider how Rosie's future in the story compares with that which you had predicted for her from the statements.

# Choices and Intentions

All writers have choices and make decisions when writing. They also have intentions that may be simple or complex. However, the intention to write a particular kind of text does not mean that readers will necessarily read in the way intended by the writer. It may be that, as a result of decisions made by the writer, readers interpret the text in ways that are quite alien to the intentions of the writer.

In the two stories that you have just read, the writers present the young Katie and Rosie as girls who are not content with the roles expected of them. They challenge and, in some ways, defy the rules. However, their rebellion is presented as short-lived. By adulthood, both girls appear to have accepted conventional gender roles. Rosie has a comfortable married life, and Katie is back in the kitchen cooking and cleaning.

It may be that girls like Rosie and Katie would not have had much choice about how they lived their adult lives. Both girls, we are told, are working-class, living at times when the class system denied choice to most people of Rosie's and Katie's backgrounds. Marriage—a "good" one in Rosie's case, and being a housewife in spite of disliking housework as Katie does—may well have provided the best future life either girl could have hoped for.

However the writers do not say this. Neither Sid Chaplin nor William Saroyan write about why Katie and Rosie stop rebelling. There are gaps or silences in both stories at this point. The "tomboyishness" of Rosie, her refusal to "behave like a girl," and Katie's unwillingness to accept the usual role of a working-class girl, at home and at work, appear to simply end when they are adults. In both these stories it seems that challenging gender and class role expectations is something that only young girls do.

## For Discussion

1. Compare what you predicted for Katie and Rosie with their futures as stated or implied by their authors. Were the futures "given" to Rosie and Katie by William Saroyan and Sid Chaplin:

   ■ more or less what you expected?
   ■ not what you expected?
   ■ disappointing in terms of what you expected?
   ■ inconsistent in terms of what you expected?
   ■ indicative of social realities?

   Be prepared to give your reasons.

2. Do you think that Sid Chaplin and William Saroyan intend to suggest that questioning gender and class role expectations is something that girls grow out of? Or, do you think that they are simply unaware of this possible reading of their stories? That is, are they unaware of the possible implications of presenting Katie's and Rosie's futures as they do?

# For Writing

1.  In both stories there is a gap of several years that the writer does not attempt to account for. Choose one of the following:

■ Write another episode in Katie's story which explains what became of her after she left her job and returned home. What decisions did she make, how did she make them, how did they lead to her situation at the beginning of the story?

■ From rebellious "tomboy" to beautiful, married woman is a considerable shift in circumstances. Write Rosie's story accounting for this change in her.

2.  It has been suggested that girls like Katie and Rosie might not have had much choice about what they did as women.

Rewrite Katie's or Rosie's future, using what you know about them and their circumstances to determine how you think they might act. For instance, one of the reasons for Katie's outrage about the guests of "the swanks" at the Great House was their sense of superiority and their lack of understanding of the working class. Could Katie have become a political activist? Rosie is determined to prove that she is the equal of the boys; could she have become a feminist?

# Interviews and Role Plays

Although the writers give us instances of the personalities and thinking processes of Katie and Rosie as young girls, there are no such insights as they become older. Use the following steps to plan joint interviews with Katie and Rosie in role.

1.  In groups, plan questions that you would like to ask of Katie or Rosie about their lives, the events they experience, and the decisions they make which lead to Rosie's marriage and Katie's return to domestic work for her family.

2.  Swap your questions with another group working on the same character. Assuming the role of that character, prepare answers to the questions of the other group. Identify one group member who is willing to take on the role in an interview.

3.  Whole class activity: Select one student to play Katie and another to play Rosie. Return all questions to the groups that originally planned them. Conduct a joint interview with "Katie" and "Rosie," directing questions to the appropriate character. It may be useful to change the students who are in role partway through the activity.

Note any responses that seem inconsistent with the character as presented in the story, or any courses of action which seem inconsistent with the time in which the character lives. These may be useful for further discussion or writing, or you could choose one of the following topics for writing.

1. For girls such as Katie and Rosie, life choices were limited. Examine those choices and comment on the choices made by Katie and Rosie.

2. In both stories, the writers present the events as entertaining anecdotes. Discuss the treatment of gender and/or class in one or both stories.

3. The narrative voice in both stories is male. Comment on the effect this choice of narrator has on the presentation of the story; does it account for any of the "gaps"? What difference might a female narrative voice have made?

# 3 Disruptions

- Does an unconventional structure change the way readers read a story?
- Does an unconventional structure make it harder to predict the way a story will develop?
- Do unconventional structures challenge readers' expectations about stories?
- Why do writers sometimes choose unconventional structures?
- How does structure relate to characterization, point of view and tone in a story?
- Are stories structured differently according to the time and place in which they are written?

## "A Mother's Fondness," "real land," and "Pledges, Vows and Pass This Note"

One of the many possible ways of thinking about a text is to examine its structure. Structure refers to the ways in which a story has been put together—the organization and relationship of its various parts. In order to understand the way in which a story is organized, it is helpful to consider structure by examining such things as:

- the setting;
- the plot outline of the story;
- the narrator (whether male or female, written in the first or third person, involved in the action or not);
- the use of "special effects" such as unusual punctuation or flashbacks;
- sudden changes in setting;
- juxtapositioning of contrasting points of view.

The structure of each of the stories in this section makes obvious demands on the reader. You are asked:

- to examine the structure of each story;
- to explore the demands made by the structure on the reader;
- to consider how and why such demands are made.

# Writing a Story

The idea here is for you to write a story, using one of the scenarios below as a starting point.

1. A mother is alone in the house; it is getting late and her teenage daughter is still not home from school.

2. A father is alone in the house; it is getting late and his teenage son is still not home from school.

3. A teenage school girl, who has been expelled from her class is sitting alone in a corridor at a desk doing some work on a map.

4. A teenage school boy, who has been expelled from his class is sitting alone in a corridor at a desk doing some work on a map.

Your teacher will assign one of these scenarios to your group. Once you have a scenario you can begin thinking about a possible story to be constructed from the information given. However, you will first need to make some decisions about your story.

■ To record your decisions, divide a blank page into five columns with the following headings: Characterization, Point of View, Tone, Structure, and Plot.

## Characterization

What kinds of people will your characters be? For instance, if you have been assigned Scenario 3, will you decide that your character is:

■ a renegade or a conformist?
■ always challenging authority or a victim of authority?
■ always getting into trouble?
■ from a poor or a wealthy family?

How will you construct your characters?

■ Using direct description?
■ Describing them by their speech and actions?
■ Describing their thoughts and feelings?
■ Giving your characters a voice with which to "tell" their own stories?
■ Presenting them through another character's eyes?

## Point of View

What point of view will you use?

■ Will you tell the story through the eyes of one character?
■ If so, will you use first person narration? For example: *I could see that Mary was smitten with remorse but I felt powerless to help.*

■ Will your narrator be involved in the action or be an observer?

■ If you write in the third person, will you limit the point of view to what one character sees? For example: *Jane could see that Mary was smitten with remorse but she felt powerless to help.*

■ Will you use an omniscient narrator—and tell the story from the perspective of an "all-seeing outsider"? For example: *Mary was wishing her actions undone. Jane could see that her friend was full of remorse, but felt powerless to help.* (In the third person example above the reader is only given Jane's point of view of what is wrong with Mary. Jane could, in fact, be wrong. Mary could have been bored with Jane's company.)

■ Will you use a shifting point of view and write different sections of the story in the first person through different characters' eyes?

## Tone

Tone is the writer's attitude toward the content of the story; it could be serious or mocking, ironic or humorous. What will be the tone of your story? For example, with Scenario 3:

■ What attitude will you take toward the girl? (Pity, admiration, or disgust?)

■ How will you encourage your readers to share your attitude?

## Structure

Given the decisions that you have made explicit about characterization, point of view, and tone, what kind of structure could you use to make your story interesting, convincing, or persuasive?

■ How will you order the events in the story?

■ What emphasis will you give to the story's various elements—such things as its setting, the method of narration, and the point of view from which it is told?

■ Will you use any "special effects"?

■ Will your chosen point of view be constant?

## Plot

■ What will be the main events of the story?

■ At what point in the story will you begin? (You could, for example, begin when it happens, or some time before, or the night after, or twenty years later.)

■ What will be the climax of your story?

■ How will you end your story?

When you have made your decisions regarding characterization, point of view, tone, structure, and plot and recorded them in note form on your chart, you can begin to write your story. You may find the following guidelines helpful for group writing:

### Group Story Writing Guidelines

Before writing: Each member should have made notes under the five headings for the scenario which has been assigned to your group. These notes should be detailed enough to form the basis of a story.

Group size: It is advisable not to work in groups of more than four for this kind of activity. If you have more than four members, people may feel frustrated because not enough of their ideas are accepted, or the group fragments, or more than one story is going, or some people simply opt out.

Writing: Usually only one person can write at a time; you may want to take turns in this job. Don't forget that the scribe cannot write as fast as you can talk. It's a good idea for members who are not serving as scribe to draft passages of text to discuss with group members and for the scribe to have the revised versions of these as rough notes.

If you get stuck, it may be helpful for each group member to try to solve the problem individually, making written drafts. These can then be shared with the group, modified, and incorporated into the story.

When you have a complete first draft, listen while the scribe reads it aloud straight through. When it is being read a second time, you can interrupt to suggest changes. When the group is satisfied with the revisions, it is time to write, type, or word process the final version.

## After Writing

1. When all the groups have completed their stories, your teacher will give you time to read and respond to each other's work.

2. Your teacher will then assign one story to your group on the following basis:

   ■ If you have written on Scenario 1, then your group will be assigned a story written for Scenario 2, and vice versa.
   ■ If you have written for Scenario 3 then your group will be assigned a story written for Scenario 4, and vice versa.

3. When you have received the story assigned to you from another group, each of you should make notes on *that* story under the same headings you used for writing your story—that is, under Characterization, Point of View, Tone, Structure, and Plot.

4. You could compare your notes on the story with those made by the group responsible for writing it and then discuss the similarities and differences, as well as possible reasons for them.

# "A Mother's Fondness" and "real land"

"A Mother's Fondness" was written by a Scottish student, Marion Rachel Stewart, and was first published as an award-winning entry in the *Daily Mirror*

Children's Literary Competition. The second story, "real land," was written by the Australian writer Joanne Burns and was first published in 1984.

# A Mother's Fondness _____

*Marion Rachel Stewart*

### The Mother

I began to worry and fidget by half past five. Two buses had gone by and she had not come home from school. I thought of all the places she could go to and became afraid because there were so many. My husband was working in Glasgow and my father, who stayed with us, was on holiday.

The house was empty. I was afraid. Not of being alone but she would have phoned to tell me if she was going away anywhere. My stomach turned, I felt hungry but could not eat, tired but could not sleep, tormented by my imagination.

At six o'clock I phoned her friend but she had no idea where she was and suggested I phone several people who were other schoolfriends. I phoned them all but no one knew and said they would phone back if they found out where she was. I took the car into town. There was a girl she was friendly with who lived in a house on the way to town. She hadn't a phone so I went to the door.

"Elaine, have you seen Cathie?" It was hard to speak as the cries of pain echoed through my head. I was too embarrassed to stay, I had started to cry and my eyes were red and sore. I went into all the cafes she talked of. It was no use. I went home and found myself waiting for the phone to ring. It did several times. Always someone to ask if I had found her. At nine o'clock I answered the phone for the millionth time. It was Mrs. Wilson, Elaine's mother. She said Cathie was at their house. I felt as though the greatest load had been lifted from my heart. Again I took the car and drove into town. She was very quiet and looked at me coldly. She thanked Elaine and got into the car. We said nothing but I wanted to be angry, I wanted to show how worried I had been. I knew that she would not see my anger as love for her. It seemed as though she hated me and wanted to hurt me, but I could tell as she sat stiffly and unmoved that she had no idea this was possible. I was as pleasant as I could be and she answered all the countless questions in a calm indifferent manner. I had failed. I could not get through to her. She could not see the agony I had gone through because of her. It was my fault she was as she was. I had brought myself pain.

When we got home we watched television and it seemed as though nothing had happened at all. It was forgotten, pushed away out of sight. That night I prayed it would never happen again.

### The Daughter

After school I met Caroline and as she had borrowed some records of mine I decided to go round to her house and collect them. I didn't really know her all that well but she was very easy to get on with. She didn't go to the same places as I did but occasionally invited me to her house and things like that. I didn't usually go, simply because I couldn't be bothered. I hardly even saw her because we were at different schools but when we met we had a good long chat and told each other all our news.

I didn't feel like going home anyway—perhaps it was because I was getting annoyed with my mother—well, not annoyed but it had become too tense being with her. We couldn't have a conversation without it becoming a row. I think she resented me a bit. I don't know why. It made things easier when I went out; I didn't have to face up to her. She really annoyed me sometimes because any row was forgotten too quickly, as though it was a routine, as though she wasn't bothered. Any arguments were never about anything important but she made them seem trivial immediately afterwards. She made me feel foolish and small. It was horrible, I hated it happening. I had begun to keep out of her way as much as possible.

Caroline and I had a good long talk about school and other things that worried us. We listened to records for ages in complete silence, not saying a word. I suddenly realised I had missed both buses and would have to try and get the eight o'clock one.

Caroline decided we should go to the loch until it was time for my bus. By the time we had walked across the causeway and back I had missed it.

"Mum'll go daft," I said suddenly, beginning to worry.

"Look, she's going to be anyway so it doesn't matter how late you are."

That was fair reasoning but I was hungry and cold and I thought I'd like to get home.

"No I'd better go now," I said. I left and started walking through town. I was passing Elaine's house so I went in to see her.

"Your mother's going daft, she's been phoning everyone. She was here, she was in town twice, she's even been to the police station." Elaine stopped and took my arm.

"Oh God," I said, "Oh no, you're joking!"

"Come in."

I sat down and buried my face in my hands. She would be furious. What was I going to say to her? This meant another row.

"Elaine, I don't want to go home. Can't I stay here?"

"You'll have to face up to her as soon as possible. That's typical of you Cathie, you run away from everything. You'll have to face up to it."

Mrs. Wilson came in. I was scared she would be angry too.

"Cathie I'm going to the phone box to phone your mother now."

My mother knocked on the door and Elaine answered. She stood quietly at the living room door.

I was angry. There had been so much fuss and now she was acting as if nothing had happened. I thanked Elaine and got into the car. I didn't see any point in talking about it so I kept very quiet and pretended I wasn't bothered. She didn't even ask where I'd been until we were halfway home.

There was no way I could show her how hurt I really was. She simply didn't care about me and I couldn't let her see how much that hurts. It was no good: she had already forgotten it—just like everything else.

## real land

*joanne burns*

this must be the fifth bloody time this month ive spent the day sittin in this corridor. its a real cold hole deadset. might as well be in siberia. as if theyd care all them jerks of teachers sittin with their bums on top of the heaters in the classroom all day. she said that Miss Lovall i'm puttin you out here near my office for your own good Cheryl. yeah i say theres no need to bung it on i get the picture. that will be enough she said Cheryl. here is a book of maps for you to draw. this will keep you busy. i want you to complete the first ten maps before lunch time. you might learn something. at least when you're holding your pen you might be able to hold your tongue. she goes back to her office. and ive been sittin here for ages at this grotty little table and wobbly chair. shell be real tickled when she sees i'm only up to map three. cant hack all these squiggles and lines and all this kindergarten colourin in. real land doesn't look like this who ever heard of pink and blue earth. might smarten up this joint ere on the map with a bit of me Orange Tropical Glow nail polish—just touch up this bit 'ere round the Cape of Good Hope, then i'll put a bit of purple eyeshadow 'ere on Antarctica—brighten it up a bit—sounds like a dag of a place to me—all that ice. all these countries strange bloody words they got for names some of these places. must be queer or something. this maps stuff is too neat for me sissy stuff—like making cakes and sewing classes. all that dumb embroidery. little chickens on aprons for mumsie on Mothers Day. makes you wanna spew. come on Cheryl Mrs. Cotton used to say you could stitch nicely if you try. look lady i said to her ive already got six stitches on me chin from when i jumped and fell out of the Detention Room in Primary school. i know as much about stitches as i'll ever need to know.

gees this place gives me the creeps all them teacher wierdos thinkin they know whats best for you when half the time they dont even know how to spell yr name right. who are they trying to kid. and when they played detectives trying to find out who set fire to the dunnies last week. old 4 eyes had to look up the roll to see who was in his class. really on the ball that jerk. just wait till i get me hands on that little punk Dwaynie Dickson for dobbin' me in. it was him who gave me the matches. got me a 2 day suspension and now i'm sittin in this bloody corridor. he'll be packin it when i get 'im. anyway they never found who burnt the toilet rolls in the garbage bins. geeze it made a good blaze.

i can't hack some of the guys in this school. when they hang in a group they act like Superman. but get them by themselves theyre as weak as bubble gum. think theyre really spunky calling us girls moles—if anyone says that to me i just walk up to them between the eyes and say look here jerk if you call me a mole again youll grow warts at the end of your tongue. wonder what the time is—i'm getting sick of this. guess its better than writing lines like i had to when i tried to grab my jewellery back out of old Fowlers bag. i must keep my hands to myself one thousand times. jesus that was a bastard. she had no right to take me silver marijuana leaf charm and me Sid Vicious badge. she didnt buy em. jeez it was funny when we were both pulling at her bag in front of the History class and the handle snapped and everything fell out on to the floor. the things she had in her bag. must have been at least 20 old photos. must carry all her past round with her. no wonder shes a history teacher.

when i get out of this place therell be no more dumb books for Chezza. i'll please myself, do what i like, no washing nappies and listenin to babies cryin like me sister Fay. 20 years old and she looks like a hag with them brats of kids and that slob of a guy shes married to. never had a moment to herself. naw. i'm gonna be free. travel round and see real land. not maps in books, travel round in me own wheels. not gonna have any boss breathin down me neck all day. think i'll be a semi-trailer driver. out on the road with me tranny. riding high in the cabin wearin what i like. i'll be good. got good eyesight. could drive me brother's Falcon when i was eight. took it out for a spin while he was mowing the lawn one day. dunno what all the fuss was about. i could drive bettern than all them jerks you see on the road crawlin along like they were sleepwalkin. yeah i'll get me licence real easy no risk. then one day i'll have me own truck. Chezzas Transport Company. yeah, you'll see all youse teachers—

> ooley dooley
> Cheryl Cooley
> she's no fooley

## Reflection

Discuss the following questions in groups in preparation for a class discussion:

- ■ In what ways were any of the stories written by class members similar to "A Mother's Fondness"?
- ■ How did this story differ from any of the stories written for Scenario 1 or Scenario 2?
- ■ If you had written in the form chosen by joanne burns, how would your writing have been received by teachers or other adults?
- ■ Why is "real land" read and accepted as a short story?

## Characterization, Point of View, Tone, Structure, and Plot

Now that you have read and discussed "A Mother's Fondness" and "real land," you should make notes on one of the stories under the headings Characterization, Point of View, Tone, Structure, and Plot.

If your group wrote a story for Scenario 1 or 2, you should now make notes on "A Mother's Fondness." If your group wrote a story for Scenario 3 or 4, you should now make notes on "real land." When you have finished, you should all have three sets of notes:

1. those made prior to your group writing;

2. those made on the story written by another group;

3. those made on "A Mother's Fondness" or "real land."

## Comparing Notes

In a class discussion, think about the following questions, referring to your three sets of notes where necessary.

### Characterization

1. One of the stories you are exploring will have a male instead of a female protagonist. How has this altered the story in terms of how it is assumed the character will act?

2. How do the writers differ in their assumptions about:

   ■ the social class or status of the central characters?
   ■ the motives of the central characters for following particular courses of action?
   ■ the central characters' behavior? (Were they portrayed as being active, confident, and assertive or as passive, angry, and unable to communicate?)

3. Do the writers stereotype characters or challenge conventional views?

### Point of View

1. From whose point of view are the stories told?

2. How do the choices the writers make about narration influence each of the following: characterization, tone, and structure?

### Tone

1. What is the attitude of the writers to their subject? Do they adopt a similar approach to the situation? For example, do they portray it in a serious or ironic or humorous manner?

### Structure

1. Compare the stories in terms of setting, point of view, and narration.

   ■ Is the setting similar for all three stories?
   ■ How does the point of view relate to the structure?
   ■ How is the story narrated?

2. Have any of the writers used special effects, such as:

- interior monologues?
- stream of consciousness?
- flashbacks?
- unconventional punctuation?

### Plot

1. How do the choices the writers make about characterization and point of view influence the plot?

2. How is the plot organized in space and time?

# "Pledges, Vows and Pass This Note"

Unlike the previous stories in this section, "Pledges, Vows and Pass This Note" appears to have several "voices," and it may not be obvious at first just who is saying what, or to whom.

## Who Is Speaking?

Before reading the story, try this activity. Look at the following statements and assign each to a female or a male speaker. Assume that each statement is being said to a member of the opposite sex.

1. I promised my mother I wouldn't.

2. Will you still love me when my looks are gone?

3. I want the first time to be beautiful.

4. Do you like being tied up?

5. But what if we had a baby?

6. Have you ever been kissed with your mouth open?

7. You only like me because I let you do it.

8. If you really love someone it's OK.

9. You're free to do what you want and I'm free to do what I want.

10. Do I have to come in and meet your parents?

   Compare your decisions with other members of your group.

## For Class Discussion

1. If you found it easy to assign most of these statements to a male or female speaker, why do you think this was so?
2. Were any statements more difficult to assign than others? Why?
3. How did you make decisions about where to assign each statement? Was there something about the statement itself—a word or phrase—that gave you a clue? Or did you use your knowledge of a particular culture? Or a combination of these?
4. What kinds of assumptions are being made about social and cultural stereotypes relating to gender? For example, who is assumed to be more interested in marriage?

## The Title: "Pledges, Vows and Pass This Note"

The title should give you some ideas about the writer's tone. The first part of the title refers to actions usually associated with the marriage service that society considers to be of grave importance and reverence. However, this image of sanctity is challenged by the final phrase—"pass this note"—which suggests schoolrooms, furtive nudges, and whisperings by students in the back rows. What is the possible connection between these seemingly unrelated sets of actions? Read on.

# Pledges, Vows and Pass This Note _____

*Frank Moorhouse*

Pass this note. He wants an answer. Pass this note on and do not read it. He wants an answer. Will you be my girlfriend? I like you: do you like me? Meet me after school, but do not tell anyone. Do you like being tickled? Do you like being held down? Do you like being chased and
5    caught? Do you like hiding and being found? Do you like being blindfolded and turned around and around? Do you like being tied up? Father Uncle Cousin Kin FM L JL true. What's your name? Would you like a hot milkshake? Don't use a straw. We'll all meet at the pictures and swap seats. I'll walk you home. Yes, but I have to be home by eleven. Do you
10   know what tickling the palm means? Have you ever been kissed with your mouth open? FM L MC true. What's your name? Can I take you to the school dance? Do I have to come in and meet your parents? Would you like coffee and raisin toast? May I walk you home? Yes, but I have to be home by twelve. Have you ever tongue-kissed before? I've never kissed a
15   girl like this before. I bet you say that to all the girls. FM L NJ true. FM L JS true. FM L FL true. FM L JJ true. I love you and I'll love you until the twelfth of never and that's a long, long time. Dearest. My dearest. My darling. Darling. Yours forever. Only yours. SWALK. With all the love in my heart. They tried to tell us we're too young, too young to really be in
20   love.

Please don't do that.
Not there. Not yet.
I'm not that sort of girl.
I promised my mother I wouldn't.
25    I want to do it, but I don't think now is the right time.
Marke but this flea, and marke in this,
How little that which thou deny'st me is;
Mee it suck'd first, and now sucks thee,
And in this flea, our two bloods mingled bee . . .
30    Be patient with me.
When I'm surer of my feelings.
But I do love you.
When it's safe.
I want the first time to be beautiful.
35    Had we but World enough, and Time,
This coyness Lady were no crime . . .
But at my back I alwaies hear
Time's winged Chariot hurrying near.
But we have our whole life ahead of us.
40    I don't want to feel guilty about it.
I don't want it to be furtive.
I don't want it to be something we just do.
But I do love you.
How little that which thou deny'st me is . . .
45    Love oh love oh careless love.
I'm very nervous.
Be gentle.
You must never tell anyone.
Have you ever done it with anyone else?
50    Was that nice for you?
How little that which thou deny'st me is . . .
Let's get to know each other a little better.
Had we but World enough, and Time,
This coyness Lady were no crime . . .
55    If you really love someone it's OK.
I love you and I'll love you until the twelfth of never and that's a long,
    long time.
Love oh love oh careless love.
FM L WH true.
We were made for each other.
60    But what if we had a baby?
True love has a guardian angel on high with nothing to do, but to care for
    you and to care for me, love forever true.
But that's all you want to do now when we go out.

It was different at first.
One-track mind.
65     Don't you ever think of anything else?
There's something you should know.
I can't tell you over the telephone.
I'm overdue.
Sorry, false alarm.
70     I'm afraid I have something pretty important to tell you.
Of course I'm sure.
This time I'm sure.
You're going to be a father.
How does that grab you?
75     I'm pregnant. I'm with child. I'm expecting, I'm in the pudding club. I'm
        in the family way. Bun in the oven.
Of course it's yours . . . I resent that.
No . . . I won't find out the name of a doctor.
The cold light of day.
If we love each other everything will be alright.
80     I want a proper wedding.
Well you'll have to tell them sooner or later.

We are man and wife now, even if the world doesn't know it.
Going out together. Going around together. Going steady.
Sort of engaged. On together.
85     That's all you think of now when we go out.
One-track mind.
Don't you ever think of anything else?
No, I want to see the end of the movie.
Men are all the same.
90     You only like me because I let you do it.
But I saw you with her in the coffee shop.
How could you?
I'm not jealous.
I just don't like two-timers.
95     You're free to do what you want and I'm free to do what I want.
I think it will give us time to see if we really love each other.
We'll call it off then.
We've broken up. We've busted up. He broke it off.
It's all over between us.
100    I missed you too.
The best part of breaking up is making up.
This time is for keeps.
But don't ever do that to me again, promise?
Don't you ever think of anything else?

105     You only like me because I let you do it.
         But I saw you looking at her.
         Really, I'm different.
         We'll call it off then.
         We've broken up. We've busted up. I broke it off.
110     I've given him up as a bad job.
         It's all over between us.
         What's your name? Would you like to go for a drive?
         Not on the first date.
         We hardly know each other.

115     I'll only say love and honour I won't say obey.
         Dearly beloved we are gathered together here in the sight of God and in
             the face of this congregation, to join together this Man and this
             Woman in holy Matrimony.
         My very dearest wife.
         My very dearest husband.
         Will you still find me attractive after I've had children?
120     Will you still love me when my looks are gone?
         Will you still love me when I'm old and grey?
         Will you still love me when you have to look across at me every morning
             at the breakfast table?
         A penny for them.
         What goes on in your head?
125     Talk to me just once in a while.
         It may have escaped your notice, but I live here too.
         You'd feel better if you talked about it.
         It says in the magazines that it is better to talk.
         You keep everything inside you.
130     But how could you: She's my best friend!
         But how could you: She's old enough to be your mother!
         But how could you: She's been with everyone in town!
         So it's come to this has it?
         There's a race of men that don't fit in,
135     It's a race that can't be still,
         So they break the hearts of kith and kin,
         And they roam the world at will.
         Poetry doesn't mend anything.
         I can forgive but it will never be the same again.
140     Don't touch me.
         If you won't talk to me will you talk to a doctor?
         It's a race that can't be still,
         So they break the hearts of kith and kin,
         And they roam the world at will.
145     Alright then, that's it, is it?

Alright then, is that all you have to say?
Alright then, it's come to this has it?
Alright then, you can tell your mother and father, I'm not.
Alright then, but don't expect baby and me to be here when you come
      crawling back.
150    And they roam the world at will.

## Ways of Reading

In considering ways of reading this story, it is useful to divide it into several sections or "chapters." Four possible chapter headings are suggested below:

1. Flirtation and Experimentation (lines 1–17)

2. Seduction (lines 18–81)

3. Going Steady (lines 82–114)

4. Marriage (lines 115–150)

These "chapter" headings are brief descriptions of the events of this story. It is, however, more difficult to identify characters and to determine the gender of the speakers. For instance:

■ the characters have no names apart from their initials;
■ the identity of the "speaker" of the lines is not made explicit.

## Understanding the Structure

In order to understand the structure of this story, it may be helpful to examine each of the four chapters suggested above in terms of:

■ plot;
■ characters;
■ "speaker" or point of view.

## A Suggested Approach

Open your notebook on a blank page and turn it on its side so that you are writing across the longest side of the rectangle. Your page should then be ruled and labelled as indicated below. You will be working down the chart from top to bottom, completing all the sections for the first chapter, and then doing the same for each of the remaining chapters.

| Chapters | 1. Flirtation | 2. Seduction | 3. Going Steady | 4. Marriage |
|---|---|---|---|---|
| Plot | | | | |
| Characters | | | | |
| Speaker | | | | |

## Step One: Plot

In your pairs or groups, reread the first "chapter" and briefly describe what happens in it in the appropriate space on your chart.

## Step Two: Characters

Who are the people in the first chapter? Describe them in terms of their gender and approximate age.

## Step Three: Speaker

Are the lines in this "chapter" spoken mainly by a male or by a female? You may not be able to make a decision in every instance but you should make a brief note of the line number and the gender of the speaker where possible.

## Step Four

Complete the details outlined above in steps one through three for the remaining three "chapters."

## For Discussion

When you have completed your chart, discuss the following questions, first in groups and then as a whole class:

■ How would you describe the plot of this story?
■ How would you describe the characters and their development?
■ Who does most of the speaking?
■ How would you describe the point of view from which the story is narrated?

## Extracts from Poems and Songs

The following extracts from well-known poems and songs are quoted in "Pledges, Vows and Pass This Note."

■ In your pairs, look at the extracts from the songs and poems where they appear in the story. In each case, say whether you think the "voice" is male or female.

I love you and I'll love you until the twelfth of never and that's a long, long time. (Lines 16–17 and 56 in the poem; from "The Twelfth of Never," sung by Johnny Mathis, written by Paul Francis Webster and Jerry Livingston)

They tried to tell us we're too young, too young to really be in love. (Lines 19–20; from "Too Young," sung by Nat King Cole, words by Sylvia Dee, music by Sid Lippman)

Marke but this flea, and marke in this,
How little that which thou deny'st me is;
Mee it suck'd first, and now sucks thee,
And in this flea, our two bloods mingled bee. . . .
(Lines 26–29, 44, and 51; from "The Flea," by John Donne)

Had we but World enough, and Time,
This coyness Lady were no crime. . . .
But at my back I alwaies hear
Time's winged Chariot hurrying near.
(Lines 35–38 and 53–54; from "To His Coy Mistress," by Andrew Marvell)

Love oh love oh careless love. (Lines 45 and 57; from "Careless Love," traditional song)

True love has a guardian angel on high with nothing to do, but to care for you and to care for me, love forever true. (Line 61; from "True Love" by Cole Porter, sung by Bing Crosby and Grace Kelly in the film *High Society*)

There's a race of men that don't fit in,
It's a race that can't be still,
So they break the hearts of kith and kin,
And they roam the world at will.
(Lines 134–37, 142–44, and 150, from "The Men Who Don't Fit In" by Robert Service).

### For Discussion

Discuss the following, first in groups and then as a whole class:

1. If you consider the extracts as a whole:

   ■ what view of women and of men do you think is being portrayed?
   ■ what view of relationships is being portrayed?

2. Why do you think Frank Moorhouse inserted sections of seventeenth-century poetry into his twentieth-century story?

3. How do these insertions affect the structure of the story?

■ Do they indicate a setting change?
■ Do they serve to reinforce the reader's impressions of character?
■ Do they serve to justify the actions of certain characters?
■ Are they a means of mocking characters, social conventions, and beliefs?

# $4$ Confrontations

- How do the ways in which stories are read change over time?
- Can it become impossible for readers to read some texts in the ways the stories ask to be read?
- What is the difference between open and closed texts?
- Is it relevant for a reader to question how and why a story asks to be read in a particular way?
- Do certain kinds of readings support particular beliefs or assumptions?

## The Epitaph of Sarah Lloyd, "Alone at Last," and "A Jury of Her Peers"

This section deals with three texts that are about violence. The way they are read now has changed—or is changing—from the way such texts may have been read in the past. As you read the texts and work through the suggested activities, you are asked to consider:

- the way in which the texts "ask" to be read;
- the way you read the texts now;
- the reasons for changes in the ways such texts are read.

## Sarah Lloyd, 1778–1800

It is now impossible to read the epitaph of Sarah Lloyd, who was hanged in 1800 at the age of 22, as was originally intended (see next page).

> Reader
> Pause at this Humble Stone
> (it) Records
> The fall of unguarded Youth
> By the allurement of Vice
> and the treacherous snares
> of Seduction
>
> SARAH LLOYD
>
> on the 23rd of April 1800
> in the 22nd Year of her Age
> Suffered a Just but ignominius
> Death
> for admitting her abandond seducer
> into the Dwelling House of
> her Mistress
> in the Night of 3rd Oct.
> 1799
> and becoming the Instrument
> in his Hands of the crimes
> of Robbery and House burning.
>
> These were her last Words:
>
> May my example be a
> warning to Thousands.

(This epitaph is engraved on a stone plaque on the walls of the Charnel House in the grounds of St. Mary's Church, Bury St. Edmunds, Suffolk, England.)

1. Spend a short time on your own thinking about the "story" of Sarah Lloyd. Make brief notes on:

   ◼ what Sarah Lloyd actually did;
   ◼ what happened to her;
   ◼ your reactions to her "story."

2. In your pairs or groups, share your reactions to your reading of Sarah Lloyd's epitaph.

3. How do you think your reactions to Sarah's story might differ from those of readers in 1800? You could begin thinking about this by reading the following short quotations from her epitaph and comparing how they would have been read in 1800 with how you read them now. Record your conclusions either in brief note form or in one- or two-word judgments.

   ◼ "The fall of unguarded Youth"
   ◼ "allurements of Vice"

- "the treacherous snares of Seduction"
- "a Just but ignominius Death"
- "her abandond Seducer"
- "May my example be a warning to Thousands."

4. To read the epitaph in the way it asks, what assumptions do readers need to share about sex, property, social class, sin, and punishment? A few examples of possible assumptions are given below, although they are not ascribed to any category.

- Sex outside marriage is sinful.
- Destruction of property is wicked.
- Servants should respect their betters.

## Two Readings?

The epitaph asks readers to condemn Sarah, and presumably most readers did so in 1800. Very few servants would then have been able to read, but no doubt there were employers who took comfort from the epitaph and were willing to read its lesson aloud. Most modern readers, however, find it hard to judge Sarah Lloyd as the text asks, in spite of burglary and arson still being considered criminal offenses. Readers tend to pity Sarah, both because of her harsh punishment and because of what now is seen as a lack of compassion in the epitaph's judgment of her. The "silences" in the text have become "louder" to modern readers than the exhortations to condemn Sarah and approve of her "Just . . . Death." To readers today what the epitaph most obviously doesn't say is, "Poor Sarah."

## "Sarah Lloyd, you are charged with . . ."

Imagine the trial of a young woman like Sarah Lloyd taking place today. She could be sent to prison for being an accessory to the crimes of burglary and arson. Certainly the most lenient judgment she could expect would be a suspended sentence.

1. Make brief notes of the arguments that might be presented in prosecuting Sarah and in defending her. (You may want to invent biographical details to support the arguments. For example, for the purposes of the defense, Sarah could be a first offender.)

2. Share your ideas with your group, and then discuss the presentation of the final scene of a trial of a modern Sarah Lloyd. Taking part in the scene:

- a prosecution lawyer and a defense lawyer, both of whom deliver their final orations;
- members of the jury, who must make up their minds on a verdict;
- the judge, who provides a summary of the evidence and imposes the sentence.

You need to plan your speech and consider such details as:

- the kind of voice or "register" your "speaker" will use;
- whether the speech is intended to persuade listeners/readers;
- whether the speech is intended to summarize and inform;
- the "form" of the speech—for example, whether it is a formal address or stream of consciousness (e.g., the thoughts of a jury member).

## Reflection

See if there is any consensus on how someone like Sarah Lloyd should be treated today. Can you identify the social and cultural assumptions (about sex, property, class, sin, and punishment) that underlie the arguments put forward and how they have changed since 1800?

# Murder Most Foul?

The next two stories are about murders. In "Alone at Last" by Russell Stockton, the killer is a man, his victims women. In "A Jury of Her Peers" by Susan Glaspell, a wife kills her husband.

1. Spend a few minutes on your own making brief notes on the kind of story you think each could be. Compare your ideas with members of your group, noting any similarities.

2. Then, in your pairs or groups, read the fifteen statements below and decide, in each case, if you think it might apply to a story in which a man is the killer of a woman or a story in which a woman is the killer of a man (you may feel some statements could apply to both):

   1. There is a detailed exploration of the killer's motive.
   2. The victim is not known to the killer.
   3. There is a chase.
   4. The victim is presented as cruel.
   5. The victim is presented as silly.
   6. The murder is motiveless.
   7. The victim is killed because of something he or she has done.
   8. The identity of the victim is unimportant.
   9. The murderer stalks the victim.
   10. The killer makes no attempt to get away.
   11. The victim is presented as taking chances.
   12. The victim's fear is described in detail.
   13. No reasons are given for the murder.
   14. It is an exciting suspense story.
   15. It is a sad story.

   Keep a copy of your decisions to refer to after you have read the stories.

# "Alone at Last"

The story that follows asks to be read as an exciting entertainment. It tells of a woman who chooses to stay home alone, ignoring warnings that a murderer is at large, rather than accompanying her husband and children on a camping trip. Despite warnings, she fails to have a window lock repaired, and she continues to go jogging in the forest near her house. At dusk she hears footsteps behind her that speed up when she begins to hurry. Terribly afraid and regretting that she has sent her husband and children away, she runs home, lets herself in, and locks the door. Calming down she begins to blame her absent husband for making her feel afraid, only to realize that the window is open and there is someone in the next room. At this point the story ends.

## Two Readings

Until recent years, texts like "Alone at Last" were often read solely as exciting suspense stories. They were seen as cleverly constructed stories with engrossing plots and deft, amusing characterization. Interest in such stories tended to focus on the techniques used by the writer to create an atmosphere of suspense. Often, the authors were praised for their skillful use of generic conventions and for vividly evoking the heroine's fear.

Recently, however, there has been criticism of such stories and their underlying assumptions, which readers are expected to share. These assumptions about women and violence, it is argued, have become visible to readers who no longer share them. To readers whose assumptions match those of the text, the assumptions remain invisible.

Critics of stories like "Alone at Last" now argue that it is possible to read the story of a woman's probable rape and murder as simply an exciting entertainment only *while* the assumptions are invisible. They suggest that a story like "Alone at Last" may be criticized for both of the following reasons:

■ what it *fails* to ask about violence to women;
■ what it *does* say or imply about women and violence.

First, critics of such stories would argue that "Alone at Last" accepts without question the assertion that:

■ most violent attacks on women are committed by men;
■ women may be the victims of violence not because of what they do, but because of what they *are*—that is, because they are women.

Therefore, the writer does not explore the murderer's motive or explain why the heroine is the victim: it is accepted as a "natural," believable situation that readers will recognize and simply accept.

Second, arising from the acceptance of women as "natural targets" of male violence, critics argue that it is implied in stories like "Alone at Last" that:

- because women are vulnerable they shouldn't go out alone and, indeed, are foolhardy to do so;
- women who are victims of violence are to blame for it in some way.

This is apparent, it is claimed, in the unsympathetic construction of the heroine-victim.

## During Reading

1. Below are two sets of arguments that might be put forward by different readers of "Alone at Last." As you read the story, think about whether you agree or disagree with the readings. It may be possible to begin recording your agreement or disagreement as you read.

| Two Readings: A Comparison | | |
|---|---|---|
| **Reading 1: "a clever, entertaining suspense story"** | **Agree** | **Disagree** |
| 1. Has an engrossing plot. | | |
| 2. Is a cleverly constructed story. | | |
| 3. Has deft and amusing characterization. | | |
| 4. Skillfully evokes the heroine's fear. | | |
| 5. Encourages a reading of violence as entertaining. | | |
| **Reading 2: "unacceptable, offensive"** | **Agree** | **Disagree** |
| 1. Accepts and confirms as "natural" that most violent attacks on women are by men. | | |
| 2. Accepts and confirms that women may be victims of violence because of what they are—women. | | |
| 3. Implies women are silly to go out alone. | | |
| 4. Implies women who are victims of violence are to blame in some way. | | |
| 5. Encourages a reading of violence as entertaining. | | |

2. The second area to pay special attention to as you read is the way in which the character of the protagonist-victim, Kate Steele, is presented. You could jot down adjectives and phrases that refer to her. Alternatively you could take note of relevant page numbers to refer to after you have read the story.

# Alone at Last

*Russell Stockton*

Still panting slightly, Kate smiled inwardly, noticing Mr. Broad's gaze flickering furtively over her costume of tight t-shirt and running shorts, and Mrs. Broad's cold stare. Mrs. Broad spoke. "Your husband and the children are still away, Mrs. Steele?" she asked, her pursed mouth and sour tone making it more a statement than a question. No doubt, thought Kate, the old bag had been listening over the fence to her arguments with Michael about their holiday. Her disapproval of Kate was palpable in the air between them, but Kate smiled back sweetly, first at her and then, more widely, at Mr. Broad, who flushed and smirked, uncomfortably aware of his wife's expression. Kate replied smoothly, "Oh yes, they won't be back for another week. I'm all on my own until then." She ran the fingers of one hand through her long, fair hair, looking up through her eyelashes at Mr. Broad.

His eyes widened. "I'd better come over and make sure of that window lock," he said. Seeing his wife's expression, he began to stammer. "The window lock, it's broken. Michael asked me to take a look at it. Not safe at times like these for you women, especially you being on your own." He coughed and made a great show of blowing his nose, while his wife continued to stare at him. "Er, umm . . . ," he stammered. "Only take a few minutes." Mr. Broad, still smiling in a beseeching way that seemed somehow to be directed at both women, allowed his voice to fade into silence.

God, thought Kate, I don't want you coming into my house. Not that she was afraid of his anxious, admiring attentions. No, she could manage those easily enough— was more than used, in fact, to dealing with pathetic men paying her weak compliments— but he was such an old bore and he would want to stay and have a cup of tea and then to chat on interminably. Her freedom was too precious to waste it with dreary old Mr. Broad. You could understand him wanting to get away from his battle-ax of a wife, though, Kate thought with a grin. But she said quickly, "Oh, don't worry about it, Mr. Broad. Michael can fix it when he gets back. I'm not a nervous person."

"No," said Mrs. Broad. "I can't imagine you ever being nervous or . . ." Her voice trailed off, but Kate knew what she had wanted to say. Something about Kate's lack of sensitivity or feeling. Yes, the old snoop had definitely been listening over the fence to her and Michael, but she didn't have the courage to confront Kate directly. She wasn't, however, going to let Kate off completely for being so attractive to her husband. "You must be missing your kiddies though?" she asked, tipping her head to one side and simpering slightly at the mention of the children.

"Terribly," said Kate flatly. She stretched her slim, tanned arms over her head, enjoying Mr. Broad's intake of breath as he glimpsed her taut midriff, as well as Mrs. Broad's look of quiet fury. "I'd better get inside, I guess. Lots to do. Bye for now." I wouldn't like to be in his shoes, she thought, as the elderly couple walked towards their gate. Kate laughed: a big, free laugh.

Inside, she leaned her back against the door, reveling in the silence and solitude. It was exactly what she'd done a week ago when Michael, along with Sophie and James, had said their goodbyes, finally, after so many delays that she'd felt like screaming, and climbed into the car loaded with camping equipment. Almost immediately, though, on that occasion, the doorbell had rung once again. It was six-year-old Sophie: "One more kiss, Mummy, just one more kiss." Then, of course, James, always having to copy his big sister, was out of the car and hugging her too. For a moment, it looked as if Michael would join in until her glare had stopped his approach. "For Christ's sake, Mike, can't you just get going. At this rate you'll arrive in the dark." Michael's slightly chubby face had colored. "OK, kids, let's go. All on board for the great outdoors." Kate winced with irritation at his jolly tone. But even then, seeing her all-too-visible impatience, he'd tried again. Smiling in a way that he seemed to imagine was appealing, he crooned, "There's not any chance of you changing your mind, sweetie? We'll all miss you, and I don't like to think of you in the house on your own, not with the attacks—" She'd interrupted him with a shout: "Michael, we've already discussed this! I want, I need, to be on my own."

Looking dashed, he'd stumbled back to the car, holding up one hand beseechingly. "OK, OK, sweetie. Bye bye, sweetie. Have a nice rest. Wave to Mummy, Sophie, James." It had been the last exchange in a month of similar exchanges. She had won. Finally, she had convinced Michael that he, who after all had been the one to want children anyway, and who was always wanting to go on family camping holidays, should take Sophie and James away for two weeks, leaving her here in the house alone.

Alone. She breathed in deeply, luxuriating in the sense of a whole day ahead, hers to do with as she pleased. No children making demands and no Michael shambling apologetically around the house like some good-natured Saint Bernard desperate for a pat. He was a nice man, she knew that; in fact it was one of the reasons she'd married him so soon after the breakup with Sam, when she'd known that if she couldn't have him it didn't much matter who it was. But it was only one of the reasons. Marrying Michael had also had the advantage of showing Sam how little she'd cared about his breaking off their relationship. And Michael was available, too. Terribly, obviously available. He had been Sam's best friend, and so Kate had not only known him for years but also known that he loved her in a silent, long-suffering way, typical of Michael, because of course you wouldn't come on to a best friend's girl. Even if he had, Kate had always known that she would be able to handle him. Sam, in fact, was the only man ever that she'd not been able to manage.

When she and Sam had split, Michael had been pathetically grateful for her attention; couldn't believe his luck, in fact. Kate had more or less had to seduce him, and, embarrassingly, he'd almost cried when she agreed to marry him. In all of their wedding photographs, while she stared out at the camera with a slightly amused expression, Michael gazed adoringly at her. What Kate had not counted on, had not been able to foresee, however, was the tedium of Michael's relentless devotion and the surprising steadiness of his determined longing for a family. When Sophie and James were born—or "came along," as Michael put it—he seemed like a man whose every dream had been fulfilled. Kate had managed, of course. In spite of Michael's doubts and misgivings, she'd promptly organized minders for the children and arranged to go back to work as early as possible, reassuring Michael by pointing out that the extra money would pay for the best schools for Sophie and James when they were older.

The past ten days had felt like heaven to Kate. While Michael and Sophie and James had teamed up with other families at the campsite for barbecues, beach games, and excursions on boats—which they tried to tell her about in excruciating detail during their too-frequent phone calls—Kate had followed a blissfully solitary routine. Each day she'd awoken with the delicious realization of being alone and had risen early to take advantage of every hour. She'd gone running every morning, and at night, too, leaving and returning home with a deep sense of satisfaction in her solitude. The house backed onto a large park that ran into a leafy forest marked only by rarely used walkers' trails along which Kate jogged. Sometimes she saw someone, like that young man she'd noticed again this morning, watching her confident, powerful stride, but usually the forest was hers alone.

During the days on her own since Michael and the children had finally departed, Kate had been content not to contact friends, although she had not been entirely able to avoid meeting people she knew when she went to the fruit and vegetable market or to pick up milk and the newspaper. Earlier that day, she'd even run into Sam and his wife, pregnant yet again, and had noticed how Sam's eyes had slipped admiringly over her figure. "You're looking well," he'd said. Kate had been light and flippant as she always was and refused their invitation to stop for a coffee. She had better ways to spend her time than sitting talking about when the next baby was due while being interrupted by the cries of their other undisciplined children who already were smeared in whatever unsuitable food they'd been eating. Not bothering to make excuses, she'd simply said, "No thanks," enjoying their surprise and the brief look of annoyance that had crossed Sam's face.

The phone had begun ringing twenty minutes after Kate, weighed down with her shopping, had let herself back into the house, put things away, and settled with a cup of freshly brewed coffee to read the paper. It was Michael, of course. His timing was always wrong, even at long distance.

"Sweetie," he'd begun, "we think we might head back today. The kids are missing you, and that would give us a few family days together before going back to work. We could be back by tonight."

But she'd known that it wouldn't be the children who were missing her. She had heard the excitement in their voices as they shouted about swimming with Tommy and cooking their food on the barbecue and even, god help us Kate thought, singsongs around the campfire. Even Michael's prompting couldn't get them to deliver convincing claims to missing her. No, it would be Michael who was missing her if it was any of them. But it was more than that, she thought, because to her surprise it had been clear he was enjoying their holiday, too. No, it would be the morning's headlines that had prompted this call—Michael's sense of responsibility for "the little woman." Another victim living over in Falconer, only about three miles away, had been found. Around the body were the same curious markings that still puzzled the police; it looked almost as if the killer had dragged something over the ground on which his victim lay. This woman's husband had been working abroad and she'd been living on her own. Not hard to follow Michael's thoughts at any time, and this was particularly obvious. Almost immediately her speculations were confirmed.

"Sweetie, you have had that window lock fixed, haven't you? Mr. Broad said he'd do it."

"Oh, yes, he's been over," she said, lying.

"And do be careful about locking up all of the doors even during the day, won't you?"

"Yes, yes, Michael," she snapped. She breathed deeply. "Don't be such a worrier," she continued, managing to inject some warmth into her voice, "and don't cut the children's holiday short. They sound as if they're having a wonderful time. We'll all be together soon."

Not too reluctantly, he agreed to return at the planned time as Kate breathed what she hoped was an inaudible sigh of relief.


That night Kate ran along the trail into the forest with an increased sense of the sweetness of her solitude and freedom. The forest was beautiful at dusk, with the birds chattering in the branches. The light was soft, the sun's rays now almost horizontal illuminating some areas of vegetation in a golden glow while leaving others in smudged blue-grey shadow. The young man she'd seen at different times during the past week had been standing, leaning somehow awkwardly against a fallen log, at the edge of where the trees were growing more densely, but now she was gloriously alone in the forest. She ran on for almost twenty minutes and then slowed to a standstill to catch her breath. The sun had slipped suddenly below the horizon of the vegetation. Even the reflected light from the outside world was failing now, and the song of the birds was stilled. She looked around her, content-edly conscious of the warm air, the silence of the forest, and the sound of her steady breathing. If only it could be like this always; if only she could be on her own whenever she chose. It was at that moment that she heard it. An indistinct sound that could have been the hoarse breathing of an unidentified creature or a shuffling, dragging footstep. Her heartbeat, slowing after her run, began to speed up again. She looked around her, but the blue-grey of the shadows had now taken hold of the forest, turning what had been softly lit trees and bushes into blurred and somewhat menacing shapes.

Kate spoke sternly to herself. "Don't be stupid. It's just Michael's phone call. He's spooked me, that's all. There's nothing there." She listened intently. Nothing. She laughed out loud. Stupid of me, she thought. It is time to get back, though, and anyway I'm hungry. She thought with sudden longing of home, of the kitchen where they all sat for their meals, and had a momentary vision of the honey-toned wooden table and all of them gathered around it in a golden glow from the old-fashioned light above. Turning, Kate began to run in the direction of the house. A sudden noise somewhere to her left made her heart move painfully in her chest. She stopped and listened. Again nothing, but then a slow but insistent rasping sound that now seemed to be a combination of stertorous breathing and the dragging shuffle of feet. The sound moved closer to her.

"Who's there?" Kate's voice sounded high and uncertain even to herself. She began to run again toward home, but suddenly all light seemed to have disappeared. The pathway, which had always been so clear and easy to follow, was now indistinct, and she felt increasingly uncertain of the direction in which to run. Normally by now she could see the lights of the houses on the other side of the park, but she could see nothing. The wind had risen too and the dark arms of the trees swished back and forth making a mournful moan, above which Kate could hear the insistent sound of what she now knew were footsteps following hers. There was something odd about them, though: there appeared to be one heavy footfall and then a dragging sound as though the person was carrying something or had one damaged leg. It didn't slow the progress of the sound, however. Whatever it was, was moving quickly. Occasionally there was the loud retort of a twig or branch snapping and then the continued sound of movement getting closer; always, always closer.

Her breath coming in ragged gasps, Kate crashed into the vegetation in front of her; the pathway seemed to have disappeared. Bushes and branches pulled at her clothes and scratched at her skin as she ran without really knowing where she was going. Sobbing now, wishing only for Michael and the children and for home, Kate blundered on through the undergrowth. Dimly aware that she was out of control and that she should try to master her emotions, she was completely unable to think rationally. Panic had taken her over completely and now all she could think of was home.

Suddenly before her, Kate saw a light, and then another, and realized she was out of the trees and into the broad open space of the park. Relief giving her extra strength, she began to run as she knew how: limbs moving cleanly, her head back, lungs taking in oxygen smoothly. She covered ground easily, almost liquidly, feeling that she was almost home, where she knew she wanted to be. "Please . . . Michael, Sophie, James . . . " she repeated their names like a mantra as she ran. She could hear nothing now except her own voice; even the sound of the wind had dropped. Then she was nearing the house and she could see the path and the kids' swings and the light from the kitchen window over the kitchen table. She could almost see Michael and the children there, but knew they were not. She muttered a list of instructions to herself: find the key, unlock the door. But her body was slow to obey; her trembling hands dropped the keys and then struggled to find the keyhole. She looked fearfully behind her and then further around at the garden and the park beyond. Bathed in the lights from her own home and those of her neighbors, it was deserted, familiar, safe—no one was there. She opened the door and went inside.

Exhausted, Kate leaned against the door. She began to laugh weakly. How silly she'd been, allowing herself to be afraid like that, imagining all sorts of things. She stood erect from her slumped position against the door, breathing in deeply, willing herself back into control. How utterly stupid to have wanted to give up these last few days of freedom, too. She laughed again more strongly at the sentimentality of her visions of the family around the kitchen table. "I've been living with Michael for too long," she thought wryly. Irritation was taking the place of fear. It was his phone call that made me afraid in the first place, she thought angrily. He and the children would be back all too soon, probably pestering her for singsongs. Moving toward the kitchen, she thought with pleasure of the solitary evening ahead of her: a nice meal , a glass of wine, and a good book without any interruptions.

Now smiling, bottle in hand, Kate reached into the kitchen cupboard. "To me!" she said aloud, raising her glass. It was at the precise moment that she tipped back her head to take a mouthful of the very good red she had poured herself that she noticed the open window and heard the sound in the next room of something dragging across the floor toward her. Simultaneously Kate realized that she'd never ever before felt so completely alone.

## Reflection

### Individually

1. Complete your "Two Readings" chart.

2. Complete the notes on Kate Steele you began while reading the story.

### In Your Groups

1. Compare and discuss your completed charts.

2. Prepare a brief statement on how Kate Steele is presented and how readers are encouraged to see her, and consider how your reading of the story might be affected if Kate Steele were:

■ alone, but not by choice?
■ a doting mother whose children were away at a school camp?

### In Whole Class Discussion

1. Share your conclusions.

2. Try to decide:

■ how you think the story "asks" to be read;
■ why it invites such a reading;
■ how you read it.

# "A Jury of Her Peers"

**jury** *n.* a body of persons sworn to render a verdict in a court of justice
**peer** *n.* a person's equal in rank or merit

"A Jury of Her Peers" is the story of a wife's murder of her husband. It was written by an American, Susan Glaspell, and has a history of changed readings.

When first published in 1917, it received criticism for its "unsympathetic" portrayal of the male characters and for its "undermining" of the law. Then, for almost thirty years, it was largely forgotten, and it was not widely available in print again until the 1970s. Since then it has become relatively popular. Here is an extract from the story:

> We live close together, and we live far apart. We all go through the same things—it's all just a different kind of the same thing! If it weren't—why do you and I *understand*? Why do we *know*—what we know this minute?

▪ Briefly discuss the passage. Try to say what you think is being talked about, who is speaking, and to whom.

## A Jury of Her Peers _____

*Susan Glaspell*

When Martha Hale opened the storm-door and got a cut of the north wind, she ran back for her big woolen scarf. As she hurriedly wound that round her head her eye made a scandalized sweep of her kitchen. It was no ordinary thing that called her away—it was probably farther from ordinary than anything that had ever happened in Dickson County. But what her eye took in was that her kitchen was in no shape for leaving: her bread all ready for making, half the flour sifted and half unsifted.

She hated to see things half done; but she had been at that when the team from town stopped to get Mr. Hale, and then the sheriff came running in to say his wife wished Mrs. Hale would come too—adding, with a grin, that he guessed she was getting scarey and wanted another woman along. So she had dropped everything right where it was.

"Martha!" now came her husband's impatient voice. "Don't keep folks waiting out here in the cold."

She again opened the storm-door, and this time joined the three men and the one woman waiting for her in the big two-seater buggy.

After she had the robes tucked around her she took another look at the woman who sat beside her on the back seat. She had met Mrs. Peters the year before at the county fair, and the thing she remembered about her was that she didn't seem like a sheriff's wife. She was small and thin and didn't have a strong voice. Mrs. Gorman, sheriff's wife before Gorman went out and Peters came in, had a voice that some-how seemed to be backing up the law with every word. But if Mrs. Peters didn't look like a sheriff's wife, Peters made it up in looking like a sheriff—a heavy man with a big voice, who was particularly genial with the law-abiding, as if to make it plain that he knew the difference between criminals and non-criminals. And right there it came into Mrs. Hale's mind, with a stab, that this man who was so pleasant and lively with all of them was going to the Wrights' now as sheriff.

"The country's not very pleasant this time of year," Mrs. Peters at last ventured, as if she felt they ought to be talking as well as the men.

Mrs. Hale scarcely finished her reply, for they had gone up a little hill and could see the Wright place now, and seeing it did not make her feel like talking. It looked very lonesome this cold March morning. It had always been a lonesome-looking place. It was down in a hollow, and the poplar trees around it were lonesome-looking trees. The men were looking at it and talking about what had happened. The county attorney was bending to one side of the buggy, and kept looking steadily at the place as they drew up to it.

"I'm glad you came with me," Mrs. Peters said nervously, as the two women were about to follow the men in through the kitchen door.

Even after she had her foot on the doorstep, her hand on the knob, Martha Hale had a moment of feeling she could not cross that threshold. And the reason it seemed she couldn't cross it now was simply because she hadn't crossed it before. Time and time again it had been in her mind, "I ought to go over and see Minnie Foster"—she still thought of her as Minnie Foster, though for twenty years she had been Mrs. Wright. And then there was always something else to do and Minnie Foster would go from her mind. But *now* she could come.

The men went over to the stove. The women stood close together by the door. Young Henderson, the county attorney, turned around and said, "Come up to the fire, ladies."

Mrs. Peters took a step forward, then stopped. "I'm not—cold," she said.

And so the two women stood by the door, at first not even so much as looking around the kitchen.

The men talked for a minute about what a good thing it was the sheriff had sent his deputy out that morning to make a fire for them, and then Sheriff Peters stepped back from the stove, unbuttoned his outer coat, and leaned his hands on the kitchen table in a way that seemed to mark the beginning of official business. "Now, Mr. Hale," he said in a sort of semi-official voice, "before we move things about, you tell Mr. Henderson just what you saw when you came here yesterday morning."

The county attorney was looking around the kitchen.

"By the way," he said, "has anything been moved?" He turned to the sheriff. "Are things just as you left them yesterday?"

Peters looked from cupboard to sink: from that to a small worn rocker a little to one side of the kitchen table.

"It's just the same."

"Somebody should have been left here yesterday," said the county attorney.

"Oh—yesterday," returned the sheriff, with a little gesture as of yesterday having been more than he could bear to think of. "When I had to send Frank to Morris Center for that man who went crazy—let me tell you, I had my hands full *yesterday*.

"I knew you could get back from Omaha by to-day, George, and as long as I went over everything myself—"

"Well, Mr. Hale," said the county attorney, in a way of letting what was past and gone go, "tell just what happened when you came here yesterday morning."

Mrs. Hale, still leaning against the door, had that sinking feeling of the mother whose child is about to speak a piece. Lewis often wandered along and got things mixed up in a story. She hoped he would tell this straight and plain, and not say unnecessary things that would just make things harder for Minnie Foster. He didn't begin at once, and she noticed that he looked queer—as if standing in that kitchen and having to tell what he had seen there yesterday morning made him almost sick.

"Yes, Mr. Hale?" the county attorney reminded.

"Harry and I had started to town with a load of potatoes," Mrs. Hale's husband began.

Harry was Mrs. Hale's oldest boy. He wasn't with them now, for the very good reason that those potatoes never got to town yesterday and he was taking them this morning, so he hadn't been home when the sheriff stopped to say he wanted Mr. Hale to come over to the Wright place to tell the county attorney his story there, where he could point it all out. With all Mrs. Hale's other emotions came the fear now that Harry wasn't dressed warm enough—they hadn't any of them realized how that north wind would bite.

"We come along this road," Hale was going on, with a motion of his hand to the road over which they had just come, "and as we got in sight of the house I says to Harry, 'I'm goin' to see if I can't get John Wright to take a telephone.' You see," he explained to Henderson, "unless I can get somebody to go in with me they won't come out this branch road except for a price *I* can't pay. I'd spoke to Wright about it once before; but he put me off, saying folks talked too much anyway, and all he asked was peace and quiet—guess you know about how much he talked himself. But I thought maybe if I went to the house and talked about it before his wife, and said all the women-folks liked telephones, and that in this lonesome stretch of road it would be a good thing—well, I said to Harry that that was what I was going to say—though I said at the same time that I didn't know as what his wife wanted made much difference to John—"

Now, there he was!—saying things he didn't need to say. Mrs. Hale tried to catch her husband's eye, but fortunately the county attorney interrupted with: "Let's talk about that a little later, Mr. Hale. I do want to talk about that, but I'm anxious now to get along to just what happened when you got here."

When he began this time, it was very deliberately and carefully:

"I didn't see or hear anything. I knocked at the door. And still it was all quiet inside. I knew they must be up—it was past eight o'clock. So I knocked again, louder, and I thought I heard somebody say 'come in'. I wasn't sure—I'm not sure yet. But I opened the door—this door," jerking a hand toward the door by which the two women stood, "and there, in that rocker"—pointing to it—"sat Mrs. Wright."

Everyone in the kitchen looked at the rocker. It came into Mrs. Hale's mind that that rocker didn't look in the least like Minnie Foster—the Minnie Foster of twenty years before. It was a dingy red, with wooden rungs up the back, and the middle rung gone, and the chair sagged to one side.

"How did she—look?" the county attorney was inquiring.

"Well," said Hale, "she looked—queer."

"How do you mean—queer?"

As he asked it he took out a note-book and pencil. Mrs. Hale did not like the sight of that pencil. She kept her eye fixed on her husband, as if to keep him from saying unnecessary things that would go into that note-book and make trouble.

Hale did speak guardedly, as if the pencil had affected him too.

"Well, as if she didn't know what she was going to do next. And kind of—done up."

"How did she seem to feel about your coming?"

"Why, I don't think she minded—one way or the other. She didn't pay much attention. I said, 'How do, Mrs. Wright? It's cold, ain't it?' And she said, 'Is it?'—and went on pleating at her apron.

"Well, I was surprised. She didn't ask me to come up to the stove, or to sit down, but just set there, not even lookin' at me. And so I said: 'I want to see John.'

"And then she—laughed. I guess you could call it a laugh.

"I thought of Harry and the team outside, so I said, a little sharp, 'Can I see John?' 'No,' says she—kind of dull like. 'Ain't he home?' says I. Then she looked at me. 'Yes,' says she, 'he's home.' 'Then why can't I see him?' I asked her, out of patience with her now. ''Cause he's dead,' says she, just as quiet and dull—and fell to pleatin' her apron. 'Dead?' says I, like you do when you can't take in what you've heard.

"She just nodded her head, not getting a bit excited, but rockin' back and forth.

"'Why—where is he?' says I, not knowing *what* to say.

"She just pointed upstairs—like this"—pointing to the room above.

"I got up with the idea of going up there myself. By this time I—didn't know what to do. I walked from there to here; then I says: 'Why, what did he die of?' 'He died of a rope around his neck,' says she; and just went on pleatin' at her apron."

Hale stopped speaking, and stood staring at the rocker, as if he were still seeing the woman who had sat there the morning before. Nobody spoke; it was as if every one were seeing the woman who had sat there the morning before.

"And what did you do then?" the county attorney at last broke the silence.

"I went out and called Harry. I thought I might—need help. I got Harry in, and we went upstairs." His voice almost fell to a whisper. "There he was—lying over the—"

"I think I'd rather have you go into that upstairs," the county attorney interrupted, "where you can point it all out. Just go on now with the rest of the story."

"Well, my first thought was to get that rope off. It looked—"

He stopped, his face twitching.

"But Harry, he went up to him, and he said, 'No, he's dead all right, and we'd better not touch anything.' So we went downstairs.

"She was still sitting that same way. 'Has anybody been notified?' I asked. 'No,' says she, unconcerned.

"'Who did this, Mrs. Wright?' said Harry. He said it business-like, and she stopped pleatin' at her apron. 'I don't know,' she says. 'You don't *know*?' says Harry. 'Weren't you sleepin' in bed with him?' 'Yes,' says she, 'but I was on the inside.' 'Somebody slipped a rope round his neck and strangled him, and you didn't wake up?' says Harry. 'I didn't wake up,' she said after him.

"We may have looked as if we didn't see how that could be, for after a minute she said, 'I sleep sound.'

"Harry was going to ask her more questions, but I said maybe that weren't our business; maybe we ought to let her tell her story first to the coroner or the sheriff. So Harry went fast as he could over to High Road—the Rivers' place, where there's a telephone."

"And what did she do when she knew you had gone for the coroner?" The attorney got his pencil in his hand all ready for writing.

"She moved from that chair to this one over here"—Hale pointed to a small chair in the corner—"and just sat there with her hands held together and looking down. I got the feeling that I ought to make some conversation, so I said I had come in to see if John wanted to put in a telephone; and at that she started to laugh, and then she stopped and looked at me—scared."

At the sound of a moving pencil the man who was telling the story looked up.

"I dunno—maybe it wasn't scared," he hastened; "I wouldn't like to say it was. Soon Harry got back, and then Dr. Lloyd came, and you, Mr. Peters, and so I guess that's all I know that you don't."

He said that last with relief, and moved a little, as if relaxing. Every one moved a little. The county attorney walked towards the stair door.

"I guess we'll go upstairs first—then out to the barn and around there."

He paused and looked around the kitchen.

"You're convinced there was nothing important here?" he asked the sheriff. "Nothing that would—point to any motive?"

The sheriff too looked all around, as if to re-convince himself.

"Nothing here but kitchen things," he said, with a little laugh for the insignificance of kitchen things.

The county attorney was looking at the cupboard—a peculiar, ungainly structure, half closet and half cupboard, the upper part of it being built in the wall, and the lower part just the old-fashioned kitchen cupboard. As if its queerness attracted him, he got a chair and opened the upper part and looked in. After a moment he drew his hand away sticky.

"Here's a nice mess," he said resentfully.

The two women had drawn nearer, and now the sheriff's wife spoke.

"Oh—her fruit," she said, looking to Mrs. Hale for sympathetic understanding. She turned back to the county attorney and explained: "She worried about that when it turned so cold last night. She said the fire would go out and her jars might burst."

Mrs. Peters' husband broke into a laugh.

"Well, can you beat the woman! Held for murder, and worrying about her preserves!"

The young attorney set his lips.

"I guess before we're through with her she may have something more serious than preserves to worry about."

"Oh, well," said Mrs. Hale's husband, with good-natured superiority, "women are used to worrying over trifles."

The two women moved a little closer together. Neither of them spoke. The county attorney seemed suddenly to remember his manners—and think of his future.

"And yet," said he, with the gallantry of a young policeman, "for all their worries, what would we do without ladies?"

The women did not speak, did not unbend. He went to the sink and began washing his hands. He turned to wipe them on the roller towel—whirled it for a cleaner place.

"Dirty towels! Not much of a housekeeper, would you say, ladies?"

He kicked his foot against some dirty pans under the sink.

"There's a great deal of work to be done on a farm," said Mrs. Hale stiffly.

"To be sure. And yet"—with a little bow to her—"I know there are some Dickson County farm-houses that do not have such roller towels." He gave it a pull to expose its full length again.

"Those towels get dirty awful quick. Men's hands aren't always as clean as they might be."

"Ah, loyal to your sex, I see," he laughed. He stopped and gave her a keen look. "But you and Mrs. Wright were neighbours. I suppose you were friends, too."

Martha Hale shook her head.

"I've seen little enough of her of late years. I've not been in this house—it's more than a year."

"And why was that? You didn't like her?"

"I liked her well enough," she replied with spirit. "Farmers' wives have their hands full, Mr. Henderson. And then"—She looked around the kitchen.

"Yes?" he encouraged.

"It never seemed a very cheerful place," said she, more to herself than to him.

"No," he agreed; "I don't think any one would call it cheerful. I shouldn't say she had the home-making instinct."

"Well, I don't know as Wright had, either," she muttered.

"You mean they didn't get on very well?" he was quick to ask.

"No; I don't mean anything," she answered, with decision. As she turned a little away from him, she added: "But I don't think a place would be any the cheerfuler for John Wright's bein' in it."

"I'd like to talk to you about that a little later, Mrs. Hale," he said. "I'm anxious to get the lay of things upstairs now."

He moved towards the stair door, followed by the two men.

"I suppose anything Mrs. Peters does'll be all right?" the sheriff inquired. "She was to take in some clothes for her, you know—a few little things. We left in such a hurry yesterday.

The county attorney looked at the two women whom they were leaving alone there among the kitchen things.

"Yes—Mrs. Peters," he said, his glance resting on the woman who was not Mrs. Peters, the big farmer woman who stood behind the sheriff's wife. "Of course Mrs. Peters is one of us," he said, in a manner of entrusting responsibility. "And keep your eye out, Mrs. Peters, for anything that might be of use. No telling; you women might come upon a clue to the motive—and that's the thing we need."

Mr. Hale rubbed his face after the fashion of a show man getting ready for a pleasantry.

"But would the women know a clue if they did come upon it?" he said; and having delivered himself of this, he followed the others through the stair door.

The women stood motionless and silent, listening to the footsteps, first upon the stairs, then in the room above them.

Then, as if releasing herself from something strange, Mrs. Hale began to arrange the dirty pans under the sink, which the county attorney's disdainful push of the foot had deranged.

"I'd hate to have men comin' into my kitchen," she said testily—"snoopin' round and criticizin'."

"Of course it's no more than their duty," said the sheriff's wife, in her manner of timid acquiescence.

"Duty's all right," replied Mrs. Hale bluffly; "but I guess that deputy sheriff that come out to make the fire might have got a little of this on. "She gave the roller towel a pull. "Wish I'd thought of that sooner! Seems mean to talk about her for not having things slicked up, when she had to come away in such a hurry."

She looked around the kitchen. Certainly it was not "slicked up." Her eye was held by a bucket of sugar on a low shelf. The cover was off the wooden bucket, and beside it was a paper bag—half full.

Mrs. Hale moved towards it.

"She was putting this in there," she said to herself—slowly.

She thought of the flour in her kitchen at home—half sifted, half not sifted. She had been interrupted, and had left things half done. What had interrupted Minnie Foster? Why had that work been left half done? She made a move as if to finish it,—unfinished things always bothered her,—and then she glanced around and saw Mrs. Peters was watching her—and she didn't want Mrs. Peters to get that feeling she had got of work begun and then—for some reason—not finished.

"It's a shame about her fruit," she said, and walked toward the cupboard that the county attorney had opened, and got on the chair, murmuring: "I wonder if it's all gone."

It was a sorry enough looking sight, but "Here's one that's all right," she said at last. She held it towards the light. "This is cherries, too." She looked again. "I declare I believe that's the only one."

With a sigh, she got down from the chair, went to the sink, and wiped off the bottle.

"She'll feel awful bad, after all her hard work in the hot weather. I remember the afternoon I put up my cherries last summer."

She set the bottle on the table, and, with another sigh, started to sit down in the rocker. But she did not sit down. Something kept her from sitting down in that chair. She straightened—stepped back, and, half turned away, stood looking at it, seeing the woman who had sat there "pleatin' at her apron."

The thin voice of the sheriff's wife broke in upon her: "I must be getting those things from the front room closet." She opened the door into the other room, started in, stepped back. "You coming with me, Mrs. Hale?" she asked nervously. "You—you could help me get them."

They were soon back—the stark coldness of that shut-up room was not a thing to linger in.

"My!" said Mrs. Peters, dropping the things on the table and hurrying to the stove.

Mrs. Hale stood examining the clothes the woman who was being detained in town had said she wanted.

"Wright was close!" she exclaimed, holding up a shabby black skirt that bore the marks of much making over. "I think maybe that's why she kept so much to herself. I s'pose she felt she couldn't do her part; and then, you don't enjoy things when you feel shabby. She used to wear pretty clothes and be lively—when she was Minnie

Foster, one of the town girls, singing in the choir. But that—oh, that was twenty years ago."

With a cheerfulness in which there was something tender, she folded the shabby clothes and piled them at one corner of the table. She looked up at Mrs. Peters, and there was something in the other woman's look that irritated her.

"She don't care," she said to herself. "Much difference it makes to her whether Minnie Foster had pretty clothes when she was a girl."

Then she looked again, and she wasn't so sure; in fact, she hadn't at any time been perfectly sure about Mrs. Peters. She had a shrinking manner, and yet her eyes looked as if they could see a long way into things.

"This all you was to take in?" asked Mrs. Hale.

"No," said the sheriff's wife; "she said she wanted an apron. Funny thing to want," she ventured in her nervous little way, "for there's not much to get you dirty in jail, goodness knows. But I suppose just to make her feel more natural. If you're used to wearing an apron—. She said they were in the bottom drawer of this cupboard. Yes—here they are. And then her little shawl that always hung on the stair door."

So she took the small gray shawl from behind the door leading upstairs, and stood a minute looking at it.

Suddenly Mrs. Hale took a quick step towards the other woman.

"Mrs. Peters!"

"Yes, Mrs. Hale?"

"Do you think she—did it?"

A frightened look blurred the other things in Mrs. Peters' eyes.

"Oh, I don't know," she said, in a voice that seemed to shrink away from the subject.

"Well, I don't think she did," affirmed Mrs. Hale stoutly. "Asking for an apron, and her little shawl. Worryin' about her fruit."

"Mr. Peters says—" Footsteps were heard in the room above; she stopped, looked up, then went on in a lowered voice: "Mr. Peters says—it looks bad for her. Mr. Henderson is awful sarcastic in a speech, and he's going to make fun of her saying she didn't wake up."

For a moment Mrs. Hale had no answer. Then, "Well, I guess John Wright didn't wake up—when they was slippin' that rope under his neck," she muttered.

"No, it's *strange*," breathed Mrs. Peters. "They think it was such a—funny way to kill a man."

She began to laugh; at sound of the laugh, abruptly stopped.

"That's just what Mr. Hale said," said Mrs. Hale, in a resolutely natural voice. "There was a gun in the house. He says that's what he can't understand."

"Mr. Henderson said, coming out, that what was needed for the case was a motive. Something to show anger—or sudden feeling."

"Well, I don't see any sign of anger around here," said Mrs. Hale. "I don't—"

She stopped. It was as if her mind tripped on something. Her eye was caught by a dish-towel in the middle of the kitchen table. Slowly she moved toward the table. One half of it was wiped clean, the other half messy. Her eyes made a slow, almost unwilling turn to the bucket of sugar and the half empty bag beside it. Things begun—and not finished.

After a moment she stepped back, and said, in that manner of releasing herself:

"Wonder how they're finding things upstairs? I hope she had it a little more red up up there. You know,"—she paused, and feeling gathered,—"it seems kind of *sneaking*: locking her up in town and coming out here to get her own house to turn against her!"

"But, Mrs. Hale," said the sheriff's wife, "the law is the law."

"I s'pose 'tis," answered Mrs. Hale shortly.

She turned to the stove, saying something about that fire not being much to brag of. She worked with it a minute, and when she straightened up she said aggressively:

"The law is the law—and a bad stove is a bad stove. How'd you like to cook on this?"—pointing with the poker to the broken lining. She opened the oven door and started to express her opinion of the oven; but she was swept into her own thoughts, thinking of what it would mean, year after year, to have that stove to wrestle with. The thought of Minnie Foster trying to bake in that oven—and the thought of her never going over to see Minnie Foster—.

She was startled by hearing Mrs. Peters say: "A person gets discouraged—and loses heart."

The sheriff's wife had looked from the stove to the sink—to the pail of water which had been carried in from outside. The two women stood there silent, above them the footsteps of the men who were looking for evidence against the woman who had worked in that kitchen. That look of seeing into things, of seeing through a thing to something else, was in the eye of the sheriff's wife now. When Mrs. Hale next spoke to her, it was gently:

"Better loosen up your things, Mrs. Peters. We'll not feel them when we go out."

Mrs. Peters went to the back of the room to hang up the fur tippet she was wearing. A moment later she exclaimed, "Why, she was piecing a quilt," and held up a large sewing basket piled high with quilt pieces.

Mrs. Hale spread some of the blocks on the table.

"It's log-cabin pattern," she said, putting several of them together. "Pretty, isn't it?"

They were so engaged with the quilt that they did not hear the footsteps on the stairs. Just as the stair door opened Mrs. Hale was saying:

"Do you suppose she was going to quilt it or just knot it?"

The sheriff threw up his hands.

"They wonder whether she was going to quilt it or just knot it!"

There was a laugh for the ways of women, a warming of hands over the stove, and then the county attorney said briskly:

"Well, let's go right out to the barn and get that cleared up."

"I don't see as there's anything so strange," Mrs. Hale said resentfully, after the outside door had closed on the three men—"our taking up our time with little things while we're waiting for them to get the evidence. I don't see as it's anything to laugh about."

"Of course they've got awful important things on their minds," said the sheriff's wife apologetically.

They returned to an inspection of the block for the quilt. Mrs. Hale was looking at the fine, even sewing, and preoccupied with thoughts of the woman who had done that sewing, when she heard the sheriff's wife say, in a queer tone:

"Why, look at this one."

She turned to take the block held out to her.

"The sewing," said Mrs. Peters, in a troubled way. "All the rest of them have been so nice and even—but—this one. Why it looks as if she didn't know what she was about!"

Their eyes met—something flashed to life, passed between them; then, as if with an effort, they seemed to pull away from each other. A moment Mrs. Hale sat there, her hands folded over that sewing which was so unlike all the rest of the sewing. Then she had pulled a knot and drawn the threads.

"Oh, what are you doing, Mrs. Hale?" asked the sheriff's wife, startled.

"Just pulling out a stitch or two that's not sewed very good," said Mrs. Hale mildly.

"I don't think we ought to touch things," Mrs. Peters said, a little helplessly.

"I'll just finish up this end," answered Mrs. Hale, still in that mild, matter-of-fact fashion.

She threaded a needle and started to replace bad sewing with good. For a little while she sewed in silence. Then, in that thin, timid voice, she heard:

"Mrs. Hale!"

"Yes, Mrs. Peters?"

"What do you suppose she was so—nervous about?"

"Oh, *I* don't know," said Mrs. Hale, as if dismissing a thing not important enough to spend much time on. "I don't know as she was—nervous. I sew awful queer sometimes when I'm just tired."

She cut a thread, and out of the corner of her eye looked up at Mrs. Peters. The small, lean face of the sheriff's wife seemed to have tightened up. Her eyes had that look of peering into something. But the next moment she moved, and said in her thin, indecisive way:

"Well, I must get those clothes wrapped. They may be through sooner than we think. I wonder where I could find a piece of paper—and string."

"In that cupboard, maybe," suggested Mrs. Hale, after a glance around.

One piece of the crazy sewing remained unripped. Mrs. Peters' back turned, Martha Hale now scrutinized that piece, compared it with the dainty, accurate sewing of the other blocks. The difference was startling. Holding this block made her feel queer, as if the distracted thoughts of the woman who had perhaps turned to it to try and quiet herself were communicating themselves to her.

Mrs. Peters' voice roused her.

"Here's a bird cage," she said. "Did she have a bird, Mrs. Hale?"

"Why, I don't know whether she did or not." She turned to look at the cage Mrs. Peters was holding up. "I've not been here in so long." She sighed. "There was a man round last year selling canaries cheap—but I don't know as she took one. Maybe she did. She used to sing real pretty herself."

Mrs. Peters looked around the kitchen.

"Seems kind of funny to think of a bird here." She half laughed—an attempt to put up a barrier. "But she must have had one—or why would she have a cage? I wonder what happened to it."

"I suppose maybe the cat got it," suggested Mrs. Hale, resuming her sewing.

"No; she didn't have a cat. She's got that feeling some people have about cats—being afraid of them. When they brought her to our house yesterday, my cat got in the room, and she was real upset and asked me to take it out."

"My sister Bessie was like that," laughed Mrs. Hale.

The sheriff's wife did not reply. The silence made Mrs. Hale turn round. Mrs. Peters was examining the bird-cage.

"Look at this door," she said slowly. "It's broke. One hinge has been pulled apart."

Mrs. Hale came nearer.

"Looks as if some one must have been—rough with it."

Again their eyes met—startled, questioning, apprehensive. For a moment neither spoke nor stirred. Then Mrs. Hale, turning away, said brusquely:

"If they're going to find any evidence, I wish they'd be about it. I don't like this place."

"But I'm awful glad you came with me, Mrs. Hale." Mrs. Peters put the bird-cage on the table and sat down. "It would be lonesome for me—sitting here alone."

"Yes it would, wouldn't it?" agreed Mrs. Hale, a certain determined naturalness in her voice. She had picked up the sewing, but now it dropped in her lap, and she murmured in a different voice: "But I tell you what I *do* wish, Mrs. Peters. I wish I had come over sometimes when she was here. I wish—I had."

"But of course you were awful busy, Mrs. Hale. Your house—and your children."

"I could've come." retorted Mrs. Hale shortly. "I stayed away because it weren't cheerful—and that's why I ought to have come. "I"—she looked around—"I've never liked this place. Maybe because it's down in a hollow and you don't see the road. I don't know what it is, but it's a lonesome place, and always was. I wish I had come over to see Minnie Foster sometimes. I can see now—" She did not put it into words.

"Well, you mustn't reproach yourself," counseled Mrs. Peters. "Somehow, we just don't see how it is with other folks till—something comes up."

"Not having any children makes less work," mused Mrs. Hale, after a silence, "but it makes a quiet house—and Wright out to work all day—and no company when he did come in. Did you know John Wright, Mrs. Peters?"

"Not to know him. I've seen him in town. They say he was a good man."

"Yes—good," conceded John Wright's neighbour grimly. "He didn't drink, and he kept his word as well as most, I guess, and paid his debts. But he was a hard man, Mrs. Peters. Just to pass the time of day with him—." She stopped, shivered a little. "Like a raw wind that gets to the bone." Her eyes fell upon the cage on the table before her, and she added, almost bitterly: "I should think she would've wanted a bird!"

Suddenly she leaned forward, looking intently at the cage. "But what do you s'pose went wrong with it?"

"I don't know," returned Mrs. Peters; "unless it got sick and died."

But after she said it she reached over and swung the broken door. Both women watched it as if somehow held by it.

"You didn't know—her?" Mrs. Hale asked, a gentler note in her voice.

"Not till they brought her yesterday," said the sheriff's wife.

"She—come to think of it, she was kind of like a bird herself. Real sweet and pretty, but kind of—fluttery. How—she—did—change."

That held her for a long time. Finally, as if struck with a happy thought and relieved to get back to everyday things, she exclaimed:

"Tell you what, Mrs. Peters, why don't you take the quilt in with you? It might take up her mind."

"Why, I think that's a real nice idea, Mrs. Hale," agreed the sheriff's wife, as if she too were glad to come into the atmosphere of a simple kindness. "There couldn't possibly be any objection to that, could there? Now, just what will I take? I wonder if her patches are in here—and her things."

They turned to the sewing basket.

"Here's some red," said Mrs. Hale, bringing out a roll of cloth. Underneath that was a box. "Here, maybe her scissors are in here—and her things." She held it up. "What a pretty box! I'll warrant that was something she had a long time ago—when she was a girl."

She held it in her hand a moment; then, with a little sigh, opened it. Instantly her hand went to her nose.

"Why—!"

Mrs. Peters drew nearer—then turned away.

"There's something wrapped up in this piece of silk," faltered Mrs. Hale.

"This isn't her scissors," said Mrs. Peters, in a shrinking voice.

Her hand not steady, Mrs. Hale raised the piece of silk. "Oh, Mrs. Peters!" she cried. "It's—"

Mrs. Peters bent closer.

"It's the bird," she whispered.

"But, Mrs. Peters!" cried Mrs. Hale. "*Look* at it! Its neck—look at its neck! It's all—other side *to*."

She held the box away from her.

The sheriff's wife again bent closer.

"Somebody wrung its neck," said she, in a voice that was slow and deep.

And then again the eyes of the two women met—this time clung together in a look of dawning comprehension, of growing horror. Mrs. Peters looked from the dead bird to the broken door of the cage. Again their eyes met. And just then there was a sound at the outside door.

Mrs. Hale slipped the box under the quilt pieces in the basket, and sank into the chair before it. Mrs. Peters stood holding to the table. The county attorney and the sheriff came in from outside.

"Well, ladies," said the county attorney, as one turning from serious things to little pleasantries, "have you decided whether she was going to quilt it or knot it?"

"We think," began the sheriff's wife in a flurried voice, "that she was going to—knot it."

He was too preoccupied to notice the change that came in her voice on that last.

"Well, that's very interesting, I'm sure," he said tolerantly. He caught sight of the bird-cage. "Has the bird flown?"

"We think the cat got it," said Mrs. Hale in a voice curiously even.

He was walking up and down, as if thinking something out.

"Is there a cat?" he asked absently.

Mrs. Hale shot a look up at the sheriff's wife.

"Well, not *now*," said Mrs. Peters. "They're superstitious, you know; they leave."

She sank into her chair.

The county attorney did not heed her. "No sign at all of any one having come in from outside," he said to Peters, in the manner of continuing an interrupted conversation. "Their own rope. Now let's go upstairs again and go over it, piece by piece. It would have to have been some one who knew just the—"

The stair door closed behind them and their voices were lost.

The two women sat motionless, not looking at each other, but as if peering into something and at the same time holding back. When they spoke now it was as if they were afraid of what they were saying, but as if they could not help saying it.

"She liked the bird," said Martha Hale, low and slowly. "She was going to bury it in that pretty box."

"When I was a girl," said Mrs. Peters, under her breath, "my kitten—there was a boy took a hatchet, and before my eyes—before I could get there—." She covered her face an instant. "If they hadn't held me back I would have"—she caught herself, looked upstairs where footsteps were heard, and finished weakly—"hurt him."

Then they sat without speaking or moving.

"I wonder how it would seem," Mrs. Hale at last began, as if feeling her way over strange ground—"never to have had any children around?" Her eyes made a slow sweep of the kitchen, as if seeing what that kitchen had meant through all the years. "No, Wright wouldn't like a bird," she said after that—"a thing that sang. She used to sing. He killed that too." Her voice tightened.

Mrs. Peters moved uneasily.

"Of course we don't know who killed the bird."

"I knew John Wright," was Mrs. Hale's answer.

"It was an awful thing was done in this house that night, Mrs. Hale," said the sheriff's wife. "Killing a man while he slept—slipping a thing around his neck that choked the life out of him."

Mrs. Hale's hand went out to the bird-cage.

"His neck. Choked the life out of him."

"We don't *know* who killed him," whispered Mrs. Peters wildly. "We don't *know*."

Mrs. Hale had not moved. "If there had been years and years of—nothing, then a bird to sing to you, it would be awful—still—after the bird was still." It was as if something within her not herself had spoken, and it found in Mrs. Peters something she did not know as herself.

"I know what stillness is," she said, in a queer, monotonous voice. "When we homesteaded in Dakota, and my first baby died—after he was two years old—and me with no other then—"

Mrs. Hale stirred.

"How soon do you suppose they'll be through looking for evidence?"

"I know what stillness is," repeated Mrs. Peters, in just that same way. Then she too pulled back. "The law has got to punish crime, Mrs. Hale," she said in her tight little way.

"I wish you'd seen Minnie Foster," was the answer, "when she wore a white dress with blue ribbons, and stood up there in the choir and sang."

The picture of that girl, the fact that she had lived neighbor to that girl for twenty years, and had let her die for lack of life, was suddenly more than she could bear.

"Oh, I *wish* I'd come over here once in a while!" she cried. "That was a crime! That was a crime! Who's going to punish that?"

"We mustn't take on," said Mrs. Peters, with a frightened look towards the stairs.

"I might 'a' *known* she needed help! I tell you, it's *queer,* Mrs. Peters. We live close together, and we live far apart. We all go through the same things—it's all just a different kind of same thing! If it weren't—why do you and I *understand?* Why do we *know* what we know this minute?"

She dashed her hand across her eyes. Then, seeing the jar of fruit on the table, she reached for it and choked out:

"If I was you I wouldn't *tell* her her fruit was gone! Tell her it *ain't.* Tell her it's all right—all of it. Here—take this in to prove it to her! She—she may never know whether it was broke or not."

She turned away.

Mrs. Peters reached out for the bottle of fruit as if she were glad to take it—as if touching a familiar thing, having something to do, could keep her from something else. She got up, looked about for something to wrap the fruit in, took a petticoat from the pile of clothes she had brought from the front room, and nervously started winding that round the bottle.

"My!" she began, in a high, false voice, "it's a good thing the men couldn't hear us! Getting all stirred up over a little thing like a—dead canary." She hurried over that. "As if that could have anything to do with—with—My, wouldn't they *laugh?*"

Footsteps were heard on the stairs.

"Maybe they would," muttered Mrs. Hale—"maybe they wouldn't."

"No, Peters," said the county attorney incisively; "it's all perfectly clear, except the reason for doing it. But you know juries when it comes to women. If there was some definite thing—something to show. Something to make a story about. A thing that would connect up with this clumsy way of doing it."

In a covert way Mrs. Hale looked at Mrs. Peters. Mrs. Peters was looking at her. Quickly they looked away from each other. The outer door opened and Mr. Hale came in.

"I've got the team 'round now," he said. "Pretty cold out there."

"I'm going to stay here awhile by myself," the county attorney suddenly announced. "You can send Frank out for me, can't you?" he asked the sheriff.

"I want to go over everything. I'm not satisfied we can't do better."

Again, for one brief moment, the two women's eyes found one another.

The sheriff came up to the table.

"Did you want to see what Mrs. Peters was going to take in?"

The county attorney picked up the apron. He laughed.

"Oh, I guess they're not very dangerous things the ladies have picked out."

Mrs. Hale's hand was on the sewing basket in which the box was concealed. She felt that she ought to take her hand off the basket. She did not seem able to. He picked up one of the quilt blocks which she had piled on to cover the box. Her eyes felt like fire. She had a feeling that if he took up the basket she would snatch it from him.

But he did not take it up. With another little laugh, he turned away, saying:

"No; Mrs. Peters doesn't need supervising. For that matter, a sheriff's wife is married to the law. Ever think of it that way, Mrs. Peters?"

Mrs. Peters was standing beside the table. Mrs. Hale shot a look up at her; but she could not see her face. Mrs. Peters had turned away. When she spoke, her voice was muffled.

"Not—just that way," she said.

"Married to the law!" chuckled Mrs. Peters' husband. He moved toward the door into the front room, and said to the county attorney:

"I just want you to come in here a minute, George. We ought to take a look at these windows."

"Oh—windows," said the county attorney scoffingly.

"We'll be right out, Mr. Hale," said the sheriff to the farmer, who was still waiting by the door.

Hale went to look after the horses. The sheriff followed the county attorney into the other room. Again—for one final moment—the two women were alone in that kitchen.

Martha Hale sprang up, her hands tight together, looking at that other woman, with whom it rested. At first she could not see her eyes, for the sheriff's wife had not turned back since she turned away at the suggestion of being married to the law. But now Mrs. Hale made her turn back. Her eyes made her turn back. Slowly, unwillingly, Mrs. Peters turned her head until her eyes met the eyes of the other woman. There was a moment when they held each other in a steady, burning look in which there was no evasion or flinching. Then Martha Hale's eyes pointed the way to the basket in which was hidden the thing that would make certain the conviction of the other woman—that woman who was not there and yet who had been there with them all through that hour.

For a moment Mrs. Peters did not move. And then she did it. With a rush forward, she threw back the quilt pieces, got the box, tried to put it in her handbag. It was too big. Desperately she opened it, started to take the bird out. But there she broke—she could not touch the bird. She stood there helpless, foolish.

There was the sound of a knob turning in the inner door. Martha Hale snatched the box from the sheriff's wife, and got it in the pocket of her big coat just as the sheriff and the county attorney came back into the kitchen.

"Well, Henry," said the county attorney facetiously, "at least we found out that she was not going to quilt it. She was going to—what is it you call it, ladies?"

Mrs. Hale's hand was against the pocket of her coat.

"We call it—knot it, Mr. Henderson."

## Clues

The extract that you read before reading the story could, if taken out of context, seem to claim a commonality of experience for all human beings. As you now know, when Mrs. Hale utters these lines she is speaking as a woman to a woman (Mrs. Peters) about another woman (Minnie Foster). It is being suggested that it is women's experience which has a commonality and significance, and that it is this commonality which enables the women to "read" the evidence the men are unable to see. For, in spite of Mr. Hale's comment, "would the women know a clue if they did come upon it?" it is the women who discover the motive for John Wright's murder.

- In pairs, look back through the story, noting the clues by which you as a reader are led to an understanding of the killing and the motive for it.
- Share your findings with the students in your class. Comment on the nature of the evidence that the women discover.

## An Analogy

The title "A Jury of Her Peers" points to a comparison or analogy being made between the events at the Wright farmhouse and events in a trial. The women's discovery of the dead bird is the final piece of evidence: "the eyes of the two women met—this time clung together in a look of dawning comprehension, of growing horror." Susan Glaspell could have ended the story at this point (or even earlier, with the line, "'Somebody wrung its neck,' said she, in a voice that was slow and deep"), providing the story with an ending not unlike that of "Alone at Last." However, she continues the story, and this decision has important implications for the kind of reading asked for by the text. The following activities are designed to give you the opportunity to explore the kind of reading "A Jury of Her Peers" invites.

## The Final Scenes

1. In your pairs, reread the final three pages of the story. Then, with discussion, divide the text into sections on the basis of one of the following:

   ◼ changes in content;
   ◼ development of story line;
   ◼ shifts in the characters' perceptions;
   ◼ changes in your perspectives as readers.

2. Give headings or titles to each of your sections. Be prepared to give reasons for your decisions.

3. In a class discussion, compare your decisions on dividing points and comment on how the last three pages affect the way you read the whole story.

## A Trial

How far can the comparison between a trial and this story be taken in terms of (a) the structure of the story, and (b) the characters?

### *Structure*

The general procedure in a trial is as follows: An accusation is made, and a plea of "guilty" or "not guilty" is entered. Then comes a hearing of evidence, followed by the jury's deliberation and verdict, followed in turn by the judge's passing of the sentence.

◼ In your groups, talk about these stages of a trial in terms of how they could be related to the structure of the story. Where possible, suggest sections of the story which relate to each stage of the trial.

| Trial | "A Jury of Her Peers" |
|---|---|
| 1. Accusation<br>2. Plea<br>3. Evidence<br>4. Jury's deliberation<br>5. Jury's verdict<br>6. Judge's sentence | |

*Characters*

The "cast" in a trial includes a defendant, the lawyers for the prosecution and defense, witnesses, the jury, and the judge.

▪ In your groups, discuss which of these roles the characters in the story might take. You may decide that some of them play more than one role, or that they play none at all. You may want to go beyond the story's human characters in looking to fill some of the roles. What, for example, stands in place of absent characters? Are all of the witnesses human? Record your decisions in the form of a grid:

| Trial | "A Jury of Her Peers" |
|---|---|
| 1. Defendant<br>2. Prosecuting lawyer<br>3. Defense lawyer<br>4. Witnesses<br>5. Jury<br>6. Judge | |

# Characterization

"A Jury of Her Peers" is written in the third person. This method of narration is maintained throughout the story; however, there are important differences in how the characters are presented. These differences have implications for the ways readers are encouraged to view the characters and where our sympathies finally lie.

1. In pairs, make a list of all the characters in the story (including Minnie Foster) and then decide which of the following methods—singly or in combination— the writer uses to "construct" each of them:

▪ what they say
▪ what they do
▪ direct description by the writer
▪ description through another character's "eyes"
▪ direct description of interior thoughts and feelings
▪ comparison with a creature or object.

2. In a whole class discussion, identify the different methods of "construction" for each of the characters and explore the effect that these different methods have on how you are encouraged to read this story.

# Point of View

For much of "A Jury of Her Peers" the reader is invited to share the women's perspective—especially that of Mrs. Hale, the only character whose thoughts and feelings are directly described by the writer. It is apparently through her eyes that we see the events and the responses of Mrs. Peters and the other characters to them. This has the effect of encouraging the reader to share Mrs. Hale's point of view and to accept her "judgments." At certain points, however, the reader's perspective is altered by a shift in point of view.

Consider, for example, how Mrs. Hale and Mrs. Peters are presented in the scene that comes shortly after the discovery of the dead bird, beginning, "The two women sat motionless, not looking at each other . . . ," and ending, "She turned away" on pages 89–90. A good way to look at how point of view functions in this crucial scene is to consider how it might be filmed.

### How Might the Scene Be Filmed?

Describe how this scene might look on film. Your description should include the elements listed below.

■ The camera shots: exactly what kind of shot, from what direction, and for how long it is held. Useful terms are "big close-up" (BCU), "medium close-up" (MCU), "long shot," "wide-angle shot," and "zoom." Does the camera indicate a particular point of view?
■ Voice and directions: what the actors say, their movements, and their expressions.
■ Sound accompaniment: music or sound effects.

| Camera | Voice | Directions | Sound |
|---|---|---|---|
| Medium shot (30 secs) | | The two women sit absolutely still, staring into the distance. Heads turned slightly away from each other. | Absolutely quiet. |
| Hold medium shot (20 secs) | Mrs. Hale: "She liked the bird. She was going to bury it in that pretty box." | The two women still motionless. Mrs. Hale speaks low and slowly. Mrs. Peters doesn't look at her but turns her head slowly to look at the box. | Footsteps above. |

*For Discussion*

1. How does the presentation of the two characters in this scene differ from their presentation earlier in the story?

2. Where does the reader (viewer) stand in relation to the characters during this scene? For example, is the reader looking through Mrs. Hale's eyes during this scene, or is the reader invited to observe both women from "outside"?

3. What effect does the presentation have on how the reader (viewer) "reads" the scene?

## Oppositions

"A Jury of Her Peers" raises a number of complex issues for the reader to consider. People, places, objects, and feelings—even concepts—are presented as opposites or as in opposition to each other, producing various "resonances" or associations.

■ One way of exploring the story and the ideas that seem to be at work in it is to make a list of these opposites or oppositions. Brainstorming with a partner or in your group should produce a list of more than fifteen examples. Here are some ideas to start you off:

finished/
kitchen/
criminal/
women/
song/

■ When you have finished your list and compared it with those of other students in your class, see if you can make groups of your opposites or oppositions in any way. For example, do some refer to place, or work, or some other specific category?

■ Can you make further connections between those things set in opposition or between the groupings you produced? For example, brainstorming ideas around the following "opposition" produced these connections and associations:

Adjective—against the law. Whose law?

John Wright is not guilty in the eyes of the law.

John Wright's "killing" of his wife's spirit: criminal behavior?

Not against the law. Innocent?

Minnie Foster's murder of her husband.

criminal/noncriminal

Sheriff Peters is sure of the difference between criminals and noncriminals.

Mrs. Hale feels it was criminal of her not to visit Minnie Foster.

Mrs. Hale and Mrs. Peters conceal the evidence—is their behavior criminal?

■ From your list of "oppositions," choose the five you think are most important in the story and rank them from most important (1) to least important (5). Be able to justify your order.

## An Open and Closed Case

Texts are sometimes described as open or closed. An open text gives the reader the freedom to make multiple meanings and to call things into question. A closed text denies options and discourages questions. There are degrees of "closedness" and "openness" in all texts.

It was suggested earlier that "Alone At Last" invites a reading that discourages questions; that is, that it is a closed text. The presentation of Kate Steele in particular was criticized for its lack of sympathy and for encouraging a reading that accepts her fate as deserved or, worse, entertaining.

In "A Jury of Her Peers" no sympathy is invited for John Wright either. In fact in spite of being murdered, *he* is not presented as the victim. One reader wrote,

> The essential crime in this story, we come to realize, has been the husband's inexorable strangulation over the years of Minnie Foster's spirit and personality. . . .

Spend a short time on your own, thinking about and jotting down ideas and opinions on the following questions, before having a class discussion.

1. Who do you think committed the "essential crime" in "A Jury of Her Peers"? Be prepared to state reasons for your judgment.

2. To what extent does the text encourage you to ask questions and to speculate about possible outcomes of the story?

3. Is "A Jury of Her Peers" a text which calls things into question, or is it a text that encourages the kind of reading that limits the freedom of the reader to ask questions? (One question to consider here may be whether the presentation of Mrs. Hale is so sympathetic that the reader is pushed into accepting "her" judgments.)

# 5 Explorations

- Can texts be culturally and socially neutral?
- Can the writing of stories be affected by cultural and social assumptions?
- Can the reading of stories be affected by cultural and social assumptions?
- How can cultural and social assumptions underlying texts about similar subjects differ?
- What is textual ideology?

## "Tea in the Wendy House" and "He Said"

In both of these stories, a young unmarried woman discovers that she is pregnant; their situations, however, are markedly different in terms of race and class. You are asked to explore:

- the reading each text invites;
- the construction of that reading;
- the ideas at work in each story; that is, their ideologies.

## "Tea in the Wendy House"

A Wendy House is a small house in which young children play at being grown up. Many of the issues explored in this story are presented in its opening lines. Read the beginning of the story (below), and then, in pairs or groups, decide:

- who is speaking;
- what has happened before the story opens;
- the attitude of the main characters toward what has happened;
- whose point of view the readers will be invited to share;
- what assumptions appear to underlie the presentation of what has happened;
- what structural devices the writer might employ.

> We're very lucky. Everybody says so. Lucky to have parents who didn't throw up their hands in horror and carry on about unmarried mothers, being too young to know our own minds, etc.

"It's very lucky," said my mother, "that you love one another so much. After all, you've known him all your life. He's always been like a brother to you. Not exactly a whirlwind romance."

I said nothing, but my mother didn't seem to notice. She went on: "It's a pity you didn't wait a little longer, but there you are. Look on the bright side. You'll still have your best years left over when your children are grown-up."

■ Now listen to or read the whole story.

# Tea in the Wendy House _____

*Adèle Geras*

We're very lucky. Everybody says so. Lucky to have parents who didn't throw up their hands in horror and carry on about unmarried mothers being too young to know our own minds, etc.

"It's very lucky," said my mother, "that you love one another so much. After all, you've known him all your life. He's always been like a brother to you. Not exactly a whirlwind romance."

I said nothing, but my mother didn't seem to notice. She went on: "It's a pity you didn't wait a little longer, but there you are. Look on the bright side. You'll still have your best years left over when your children are grown-up."

"Are they the best years?" I asked. "I thought now was supposed to be the marvellous time, and we're all meant to be living it up, burning the candle at both ends, finding out what we want to do with our lives."

"Yes, well." My mother looked up from the sewing-machine. She was busy giving some final touches to The Dress. "That's true, of course, but I've always thought that youth was wasted on the young. Someone once said that. I can't remember who it was, but I've often thought how true it was. You've got a lot to be happy about. Graham's very good to you, and he's got a job, and of course there's the house. You really have struck gold there. Not so many young people start out with a place of their own. It needs a bit doing to it, I know, but it's yours. You work on it, and it'll be a showpiece in no time."

Showpiece. You wouldn't know it just by looking at it. A small, terrace house in a dingy street. No trees. No front garden, just two feet of concrete between the house and the pavement, with a little wall to separate us from the road. No back garden either. A tiny yard full of scrubby tufts of grass trying to look green, and someone's garage wall at the end. Beyond that, more terraces, and windows with grey curtains. It doesn't matter what colour they were to begin with. In this kind of house, in this kind of street, they soon collect a grey film that makes them all look much the same.

Still, my mother was right. We were lucky. Graham, articled to a solicitor well known in this town, with a steady future of respectability clearly written all over his face, had inspired the building society to uncharacteristic flights of generosity. And my parents, who, as Dad put it, "have quite enough to see you right" from the sale of used cars in Dad's showroom, had paid the deposit for us as a wedding present. And I? I had passed my A-levels very nicely, thank you, and perhaps one day, I might be able to make use of them and train to be a teacher when my own child was at school. That was what Mum said, anyway. Meanwhile, we had a house.

"You've no imagination," Graham said the other day, as we stood at the window of what was going to be the baby's room, and looked out at the muddy patch behind our house.

"I can fix a trellis to that garage wall, and we can have climbing plants all over it. Next year. And we can plant grass seed. We can have crazy paving, with those stone pots that have flowers poking out of holes. You know, sort of Spanish."

A hacienda in Grafton Road? Perhaps I could wear a mantilla to hang nappies on the line? I didn't say anything, because Graham was so enthusiastic, but I couldn't see it. I was too preoccupied with what I felt: about the baby, about Graham, about *now* to be able to visualize the future. Also, in our house I still think of the woman who used to live there. We saw her once. When we looked at the place for the first time. She seemed very ordinary. But her kitchen wallpaper, from floor to ceiling, was a mad pattern of Dutch tiles, bright blue and white, with little Dutch children in clogs stomping about happily, and cows and windmills and tulips: the works. It made you dizzy to look at it. It wasn't very clean either, so the Delft blue was spotted with grease and damp, brown in some places, yellow in others.

"We'll have to get rid of all this," Graham had whispered then and I had agreed.

We stripped the kitchen last week, and painted it. Now it's glossy cream and pale blue and beautiful, but I find myself looking out of the window at the broken slats of the fence between our house and the next, and understanding very well why canals and tulips and windmills and clear blue Dutch skies had been important to the woman who had stood in that kitchen before me.

*The Wendy House is very pretty. The curtains at the tiny windows are spangled with yellow flowers. The wooden walls are painted yellow too, like butter, daffodils and the hearts of daisies. The table is white and there are four little white stools. Inside the Wendy House, everything is comforting and bright. Inside the Wendy House, even on the dullest day, everything is bright and pretty. Yellow and white.*

"Let's try it on then," said my mother, and I stood up obediently with my hands above my head while she slid the silky materials over my arms. "There!" she breathed. "I think that's just right now, don't you?" I looked in the mirror. Perhaps not the most beautiful bride in the world, but OK. I would have been quite happy with something new from a shop, but no, I was to have a Proper Wedding dress (even if it wasn't white) and a Proper Wedding, with all the trimmings. As my mother put it: "There's no reason not to have a celebration, just because there's a baby on the way. Perhaps one should celebrate even more." I wasn't going to be cheated out of my Day to Remember, oh no, and neither was she.

This dress reminds me of my first long dress. I was fourteen, Graham was fifteen. There was a dance at the Church Hall. He asked me to go.

"I'm going to that thing on Saturday," he said, leaning against our coal bunker. "You know. At the Church Hall. Want to come?" He sounded as if he couldn't give a damn either way.

"OK." I yawned, sounding as if I could take it or leave it.

"Seven-thirty, it starts," he said, "and ends at half past eleven."

"Great." My heart was thumping. I wished he would go away so that I could go upstairs and look at all my clothes. Maybe I could have a new dress. Maybe Mum would make one. We'd walk into that Church Hall, and everyone would stand back and burst into song, like that man in "Gigi": "Why, you've been growing up before my very eyes!"

Mum made the dress. It was red and frilly, and I thought I looked terrific. Graham, when he saw me, looked me up and down and said: "You'll do." And it was wrong. Everyone else was wearing ordinary daytime clothes. They stared at me, but didn't say anything. I wanted to die. Graham, I thought, would hate me, and would never even take me fishing with him again, down on the Canal. Perhaps he wouldn't speak to me again. I danced, and went through all the motions of enjoying myself, but we left early and on the way home I burst into tears, and cried and cried and wouldn't stop. Graham said nothing. That made me furious. I wanted to hit him. We passed the tree stump that we used to play "King of the Castle" on, years ago.

"Lynn," Graham said. "Lynn, come and sit down."

I sat. I was exhausted. I'd stopped crying. I didn't have the strength to squeeze out one more tear. Graham knelt beside me, and took out his handkerchief. Without saying a word he wiped my face gently, holding my head steady with his other hand.

"I'm sorry," I whispered. "I wanted to look just right, and I . . . it was dreadful."

"I thought you looked," he hesitated, "beautiful."

I couldn't see properly in that light, but by the way he kept his head turned away, I could tell he was blushing. I loved him for saying that, for trying to cheer me up. I laughed.

"I looked dreadful," I said. "Well, not dreadful exactly. Just wrong."

"I didn't think so." He sounded angry.

"I'm sorry, Gray. I know you were being kind."

"I was bloody well *not* being kind," he yelled.

"Shh! You'll wake everyone up."

"I meant it," he whispered. "I mean it." And he bent his head so that his mouth was hidden in the folds of my skirt, and said so softly that I could hardly hear it, but I felt it more than heard it, through the red material, murmured against my leg: "I love you."

I didn't know what to do. Suddenly Graham, whom I'd known all my life, was different. I didn't recognize his voice, the way he was speaking. He looked up. His mouth was trembling. All at once, he got up. I thought: he's sorry now, he's sorry he said all that. He wants to go home. He wants everything to be like it was before. I stood up too. My legs felt shaky. Graham didn't move.

"Are we going home now?" I asked in what I hoped was more or less a normal voice.

"In a minute. Lynn?"

"Yes."

"Can I kiss you?"

I blushed. I could feel the redness spreading all over my face, down my neck, covering me. I didn't know what to say. He took my head between his hands carefully, gently, like someone holding a precious vase. I closed my eyes. He kissed my mouth, and it felt like warm butterflies brushing my lips, softly, quickly, and then it was gone.

We walked in silence. Not touching. When we reached home, we stood for a moment beside the tree near my gate.

"Thank you for a lovely evening," I said. "I enjoyed it."

"Rubbish," said Graham, "you hated every minute of it."

"Not every minute," I said, and then he took my hands and pulled me right up to him. I could feel the warmth of his body. This time when he kissed me, his mouth stayed on mine, and I opened my lips a little, and so did he, and I could taste him in my mouth.

"I reckon," he said, after a while, "that with a bit of practice, we could get quite good at this."

He was grinning. I could hardly walk up to the front door.

"Hey," he whispered after me, "you look smashing."

I went to bed quickly, even though my mother was waiting to hear all the details. I stared into the mirror, expecting to see huge marks like red flowers blazing on my mouth where I had been kissed, but I looked just the same as I always did. Lying in bed, I thought of what Graham had said: "With a bit of practice." That meant he was going to kiss me again. And then again. And I wanted him to.

That was three and a half years ago. The kisses went on. They changed in character: grew as we grew older. And, of course, after we had become used to them, we wanted more. And different. New excitement. New pleasures. So one thing, as the saying goes, led to another.

*Lynn and Mandy are playing in the Wendy House. They are having a tea party. There are teacups made of red plastic on the table, and a little teapot. Lynn and Mandy are*

*Mummies. They have dolls. The dolls are babies. They are pouring pretend tea into the teacups. Drinking it. Pouring more tea. The dolls fall over. They are picked up again.*

*A boy comes into the Wendy House. He sits on one of the little white stools. He pushes a doll over. Grabs the teapot out of Lynn's hand. Lynn bursts into tears.*

*"Go away! We don't want you!" she shrieks. A lady comes to see what the noise is all about. She understands at once.*

*"Graham! You mustn't do that. It's Lynn's and Mandy's tea party. You mustn't spoil it. Go and play on the slide and let the girls get on with their game. They're much smaller than you. You're a big boy of four."*

*Graham is taken to the slide. He looks longingly at the teapot and the tiny red cups. Lynn and Mandy are passing round pretend cakes. The babies are being naughty. Lynn is shouting at her baby. "Naughty boy! Naughty!"*

There's nothing left in my room now. All my clothes are packed in suitcases, stacked in the bedroom of our little house, waiting to be put away. Every single childhood thing that I possess, all the dolls, books, cuddly toys, the posters of David Bowie and John Travolta, everything has been collected by my mother, and put into trunks in the cellar.

"Waste not, want not," she said cryptically. "You must think of your child."

What makes her think that my child will want posters of David Bowie and John Travolta, anyway? They'll be old hat by then. They're already old hat. A child. That's what I still am to my mother. She would never say so, and I probably wouldn't think such a thing if I weren't pregnant, but pregnant-me thinks: she's keeping something of me, something of the child I was, in those trunks down there, so as not to lose me entirely, so as not to lose my childhood completely.

When I first found out that I was pregnant, I tried to run away. I didn't really think at all, not about where I was going, nor about what I would do when I got there. I didn't take any money with me. I didn't pack anything. I just went as I was and got on the first train I could find. To Stoke-on-Trent. By the time I got there, I'd changed my mind. I phoned Graham at work. I was crying.

"Come and get me, Graham. I want to come home. Please come and get me. I haven't any money."

Graham didn't ask any questions. He simply said: "Stay there. Stay in the buffet. I'll be there. I'll come in Dad's car. I'll ring your mother. I'll tell her something, or she'll worry. Wait for me."

"I'm waiting."

I drank three cups of vile, greyish coffee. They seemed to go on and on. Then Graham burst into the buffet, out of breath. He must have run all the way from the car park. He pushed his way through the tables to where I was sitting. He pulled me to my feet, and flung his arms around me and squeezed me as if he wanted to gather me right into himself, never let me go, and we stayed like that for a long time, not speaking, rocking to and fro. The other people all around us must have thought—I don't know what they must have thought.

"Let's get out of here," Graham said at last. "Come and sit in the car."

We walked in silence to where the car was waiting. As we sat down, Graham said: "Please don't ever run away again, Lynn. Do you promise?"

"OK," I said. "Don't you want to know why I did?"

"In a minute. I just want to say something first."

"OK."

"I don't know how to say it. It sounds so bloody corny."

"Go on."

"Will you marry me?"

I started laughing, and the laughter grew and grew, and Graham laughed too.

"I told you it was corny," he said. "But will you. Will you marry me?"

"It looks as if I have to," I said.

"No you don't. But I wish you would."

"Stupid! I do have to. Well, not have to exactly, but I'm pregnant, so it's just as well you asked me."

Graham said nothing. The laughter disappeared quite suddenly, out of the air.

"Don't tell me," I said. "You've changed your mind. I don't blame you. You really don't have to saddle yourself with a wife and baby at nineteen, you know. I can quite see where it would tie you down."

"I'm bloody furious, if you must know," he muttered, with exactly the same look he used to give me years ago if I jogged his elbow while he was making aeroplane models, or walked through his game of marbles, scattering coloured glass balls in all directions.

I screamed at him: "What gives you any right to be furious? You're the bloody father. Whose bright idea was it, anyway? Who wanted me so much that it hurt? Who was it told me all those things? All those LIES? Anyway, who needs you? I'll have this baby on my own, and you can go and get knotted, for all I care!"

He put his head in his hands. "You don't understand, Lynn," he whispered. "You didn't understand. I'm not cross about the baby. I love you."

"You said you were furious."

"I was. I am. But not about what you think. Not about that."

"About what, then?"

"About you running away. Away from me. When you should have been running . . . oh, I don't know, running to find me. Do you see?"

"I didn't know if you'd want me."

"That's what makes me angry. That you didn't know that. Do you really think I didn't mean any of those things I said.?"

"Well, I thought you did, at the time. But it could have been the white heat of passion, couldn't it? A madness produced by the nearness of my luscious body?"

Graham laughed. "It could, I suppose. But it wasn't. I love you, and I'll tell you something else."

"What's that?"

"I'm quite pleased that you're pregnant."

"I don't know if I am."

"You'll be a lovely mum."

"Is that all? A lovely mum? I used to have ambitions."

"Really?"

"Yes. Trapeze artist, deep-sea diver, high-powered business woman, inspiring teacher—you name it, I've wanted it. I want to sing at La Scala and dance at Sadlers Wells."

"I don't think anyone can do both, can they?"

"Don't be so damned literal. You know what I mean."

Graham smiled. "Yes. I know what you mean." He started the car.

"We're going home."

"What'll we tell them?"

"The Truth."

"Oh Lord. Really?"

"Yes, really. And Lynn? I want you to know something. I asked you to marry me before I knew . . . about the baby, I mean. I've always wanted to marry you."

"Have you? Always?"

"Well, since I was about six?"

"You never said."

"It just never came up before, that's all."

*Lynn and Mandy are having tea in the Wendy House.*

*"I'm the Mummy," Lynn says, "and you're the little girl."*

*"I want to be the Daddy." Mandy's mouth puckers up. Maybe she will cry.*

*"Silly." Lynn is scornful. "Girls can't be Daddies. Boys are Daddies."*

*"We haven't got a boy."*

*"I'll get Graham." Lynn runs to the climbing frame. Graham is hanging upside down by his knees from the top bar.*

*"Graham," she shouts. "Come and play. Come and be a Daddy in the Wendy House."*

*"Don't want to."*

*"Come on." She tickles him under the arms and he hits her and climbs down. She pulls him over to the Wendy House.*

*"I don't want to be a stupid Daddy in a stupid Wendy House."*

*"I've got cakes," says Lynn.*

*"Not real cakes."*

*"You can pretend they're real." She pushes him on a stool. "You can pour the tea if you like."*

*"I'm the baby," says Mandy.*

*"Can I put her to bed?" Graham asks Lynn.*

*"Yes." Lynn looks at Mandy. "Bedtime. Lie down over there."*

*Mandy lies on the floor. Graham covers her with a blanket. "Go to sleep, baby?"*

*Lynn and Graham sit on white stools, sipping pretend tea out of the red plastic cups. The light pours through the sunshiny curtains, and glitters on the glossy, white paint of the table. Inside the Wendy House, everything is bright and pretty.*

Lying in my bed, I think: this is the last time I shall sleep here. Every night for the next ten, twenty, forty, sixty years, I shall lie near Graham in the new double bed. My mother has slept in the same bed with my father for twenty-one years and shows no visible signs of distress, or even boredom. Will it be boring, ever? Like a comfy old cardigan that you wear because you're used to it? Perhaps one day I will feel like throwing the old cardigan in the cupboard, and long to wear something wicked: blood-red satin or black velvet. Will my daughter (because it will be a daughter) lie in her bed and think of me and Graham as I think about Mum and Dad? Did Mum think the same things about her mother? We are an endless chain of mothers and daughters, all fitting together like a set of Russian dolls stretching to infinity, and it makes me feel dizzy just to think about it.

Yesterday, we finished painting the front room of the house. We painted it white. The curtains were all ready to hang up. Mum had made them. The material, a lovely pattern of small yellow and white flowers, looked familiar to me, although I couldn't place it at first. I knew I wanted it as soon as I saw it. It stood out from all the other fabrics as if it were lit up.

My mother said: "With curtains like this, you'll think the sun is always shining."

Graham hung the curtains.

"Not bad," he said, lying back on the sofa to admire them.

"I think they're smashing," I said. "I think this whole room is going to look great."

"Come and sit down, Lynn. Come and try the sofa."

"It's no beauty."

"Beggars can't be choosers. We'll save up for a new one. At least it's comfortable."

I sat down and closed my eyes. I felt tired. All the time now I feel tired. It's the baby. Everyone says so. I felt warm, and tired and soft inside, all over.

"I'm very far away," I murmured. "I think someone is kissing me."

"You betcha," Graham whispered. "I'm kissing you. There is some doubt," he kissed my eyes and my lips and my throat and my hair lightly, gently, "that I will ever be able to stop."

"Don't ever stop kissing me. Don't ever, ever stop loving me."

"I never will," he said. "I never will."

"Graham," I said, tried to say, "Graham, we've got so much to do. Do you think we should? I mean, I feel strange here . . . please."

"It's me," he whispered, "remember? It's only me." And he kissed me, and touched me, and held me, and whispered love into my hair and my eyes.

Later, Graham went out to get us some fish and chips. I lay on the sofa and looked at the curtains. Where had I seen curtains like this before? I couldn't think, but I felt strangely frightened, and longed for Graham to come back. Why? It was going to be a beautiful room, bright and full of sunshine. It was going to be a lovely life, wasn't it? Wasn't it? I loved Graham. I wanted him. Didn't I? And my baby! I would love her. We would love her. The Dutch tiles had gone from the kitchen and I would sit at the new table and pour tea. I sat up then, just as Graham opened the door.

"Graham," I said. "I've just thought. Where I've seen curtains like that before."

"Well?"

"At our nursery school. Do you remember? We used to have tea in the Wendy House. The Wendy House had curtains a bit the same. Didn't it?"

"Can't remember, really. Here, take this off me."

We ate our fish and chips. Graham talked and talked, and I said very little.

Tomorrow, I'm moving in. Moving into my new home. Into my new life. Into the Wendy House. I should sleep Beauty sleep. Can't look awful on my wedding day: "The bride wore pale pink silk jersey and purple circles under her eyes." The bride looked haggard—the bride—the girl—the child—Graham's lifelong friend—and life is very long, isn't it? Playmate, companion, partner, till death us do part, or do us part. Which? It doesn't matter, not really. Everything is arranged, all fixed up, painted. Bright and pretty.

*There is no one in the Wendy House except Lynn. Mandy isn't there. Graham isn't there. A doll is sitting on one stool. Lynn pours tea into the red plastic cups from the small, red teapot. She picks the doll up and holds it on her lap. The sides of the Wendy House seem higher. Lynn can hear the other children talking, laughing, crying somewhere on the other side of the walls, but she cannot see them. She tries to open the small door, but it won't open. She pushes it and pushes it and the thin wood shakes, but no one comes to let her out. The walls of the Wendy House are covered in a pattern of Dutch tiles: blue windmills unmoving, children in clogs frozen like statues, unbending flowers all in hard blue, and blue and white. Where has the yellow gone? Where are the white and yellow flowers at the window? Lynn rattles at the doorknob. Shouts. No one comes. No one answers her. She can hear them, talking, shouting, not at her. She cannot get out. She goes back and sits on one of the small stools, rocking the doll. The bright blue walls seem to be closing in around her, the ceiling is coming nearer and nearer. She is happy, rocking the doll. She is Mummy. Mummies love to rock dolls. Mummies love to play in the Wendy House. It doesn't matter that she can't get out. She pours another cup of pretend tea. Inside the Wendy House, even on the dullest day, everything is bright and pretty.*

## The Episodes

You will have noticed the story within a story which tells a literal tale of tea in a Wendy House and gives the main story its title. Printed below are brief descriptions of (a) the four episodes of the "story within" and (b) the part of the main text that precedes each of them.

■ In pairs or groups, read the following descriptions of the episodes and match them to the relevant main text description.

Lynn alone in Wendy House with doll. Everything is bright and pretty.

Description of Wendy House. Everything is bright and pretty.

Lynn's thoughts about marriage and the relationship between mothers and daughters. Description of newly decorated house. Lynn and Graham make love. Lynn's recognition of curtains; her fears. Graham's feelings. New life starting tomorrow.

Lynn and friend playing. Search for a Daddy. Graham's initial resistance followed by involvement in "game."

Mother and daughter talk. Making of wedding dress. Lynn's description of future home. Graham introduced.

Account of mother's attitude expanded. Flashback to Lynn's first "date" with Graham. Development of relationship.

Little girls playing Mummies in the Wendy House and drinking pretend tea. Intrusion of a boy. Response of girls and supervisor. Exclusion of boy; his feelings described.

Mother and daughter's relationship. Discovery of pregnancy. Reactions of Lynn and Graham. Lynn's ambitions. Marriage proposal.

## What Is the Purpose of the Episodes?

The Wendy House episodes are clearly more than just a story within a story. Like the insertions in Frank Moorhouse's "Pledges, Vows and Pass this Note," they perform a variety of functions, the most important being to provide a commentary on the main text and the issues it explores. Two of the episodes also serve as "flashbacks," and one offers a metaphor for the future.

1. In pairs, reread the episodes and make a note of any lines, words, or phrases that you think encourage a particular kind of reading of the main story. In particular, look for:

   - examples of repetition (what effect does it have?);
   - direct or indirect comments on expectations of male and female behavior;
   - lines or phrases that link directly with the language or content of the main text.

2. Then write down:

   - the main functions of each episode (e.g., commentary, flashback, or flashforward, etc.);
   - the tone of each.

3. Finally, discuss as a class the effect the episodes have on how you are encouraged to read the story. (For example, how are readers invited to view marriage and motherhood?)

## Tea and Sympathy?

It has been suggested that some stories are closed. That is, they encourage a reading that doesn't invite questioning of the text—of the presentation of characters and events or of the assumptions that underlie it.

Both the use of first person narration and the inclusion of episodes that act as a kind of commentary on the issues explored in the main text encourage a reading of this story that is very sympathetic to Lynn. Although not unsympathetic to Graham, the text says very little about the effect of marriage and fatherhood on his life. Some readers might argue that it is Graham we should feel sorry for, and that Lynn should be grateful that he's willing to marry her.

### For Discussion

Talk about the following questions in your groups and be prepared to share your conclusions in a class discussion.

1. Is "Tea in the Wendy House" fair in presenting Lynn, and not Graham, as trapped by marriage?

2. Does the story discourage the reader from questioning its assumptions, for example, that it is Lynn who is trapped by marriage and parenthood?

3. Might any of the following changes to the story make it either (a) more "open" or (b) more "closed"?

| Possible Changes | Open | Closed |
|---|---|---|
| Telling the story from the third person point of view. | | |
| Telling the story from Lynn's and Graham's points of view. | | |
| Telling the story from Graham's point of view. | | |
| Removing the Wendy House episodes. | | |
| Presenting Graham as a nasty man. | | |
| Presenting Lynn and Graham as being poor. | | |

4. As well as the reading encouraged by "Tea in the Wendy House," is there another "reading" of Lynn's and Graham's situation that the story is consciously challenging?

# "He Said"

The story that follows also portrays a young unmarried woman who discovers she is pregnant, but the results are quite different. Begin considering these differences, and how they arise, as you read the story.

## He Said

*Barbara Burford*

He said:

"This is special, so special."

And he said:

"We're so close, I don't want *anything* to come between us. You can understand that can't you?" And now, he would not speak to her, would not even come to the phone. But his brother said:

"Why you let him get you pregnant, girl? Don't you know anything at all? What you expect him to do?" She stood shaking in the phone booth for a long time. Slumped against the dirty glass with the faint smell of urine around her. Realising that probably some man had walked away from relieving himself, without a backward thought of who had to put up with the results. Just like Errol. A woman in a grey mac tapped on the glass, and on getting no response from Bev, opened the door.

"You all right, dear?"

Bev did not reply, merely shoved her way past, paying no heed to the "Some people! No manners at all!" that followed her as she bolted for the sanctuary of her bedsit.

Getting up to her fourth floor room was already becoming difficult. Her bra was suddenly too tight, her over-sensitive nipples constricted and painful. Halfway up, she became so breathless that she had to stop and sit on the stairs, her head swimming.

She heard feet pounding rapidly down the arch of stairs above her and tried to get up, but her head swam, and when she clung to the banister it rocked, giving her such a shock that she subsided with a bump. Shocked at the immediacy of her fear for the child, up till then feared and unwanted.

"You okay?"

Bev raised her head and found the woman from the floor below hers looking at her with concern. "Yes, I'm fine." She managed a wavery smile.

"You don't look it," the woman said bluntly.

"I'll be fine. Just a bit dizzy, that's all." The woman was wearing her uniform, she must be on her way to work. "Don't let me keep you. I'll be fine," Bev repeated.

"I'd believe you, if your face wasn't the colour of a ripe avocado," the woman smiled.

That did it! Bev began to retch violently.

"Oh, shit! I'm sorry!" The woman got her to her feet and supported her up the next flight of stairs to their shared bathroom on the landing. Holding her while she retched till her eyes streamed, and her stomach muscles hurt from straining. Then Bev found herself sat down with gentle firmness on the stool, while her face was wiped with a warm face cloth.

Bev opened her eyes tentatively and looked at the woman who was perched on the edge of the bathtub, regarding her critically, the face cloth still in her hand.

"That's not mine," Bev sniffed and looked towards the rail, "mine's pink."

"It's mine." The woman reached over and tore off some toilet paper which she handed to Bev.

Bev blew her nose, and made a business of disposing of the toilet paper, all the while conscious of the woman's scrutiny. She was feeling better, but still very shaky, and afraid that those eyes watching her so carefully would see straight through to what was really wrong with her. She found that she could not meet the woman's eyes.

"Thank you, I'm alright now," she muttered ungraciously. "Don't let me make you late."

"I've got plenty of time," the woman said. "I'll give you a hand up to your room when you're ready."

"I think I'll stay here for a while," Bev said hastily, thinking of the state of her room. "Just in case . . ." she managed a weak smile.

"Okay," the woman rinsed and replaced her flannel on the rail, but just as Bev thought she was leaving, she paused in the doorway. "Have you seen a doctor?"

Bev shook her head, then remembered to add: "It's nothing, just an upset stomach." She didn't want it getting back to her parents. She didn't know this woman, but that was not to say that the woman did not know who she was, or know someone who would tell her father.

The woman looked hard at her, then she left, pulling the door to behind her.

Back in her room at last, Bev surrendered to tears. Crying as she had not done since her father had thrown her out. But even that massive rejection had been ameliorated somewhat by the feeling that she was enduring all that for love of Errol, that she had him, and now they could be together. Now, Errol did not want to know her, and her father's predictions looked like coming true. And there was no way back into that fold:

"My daughter is dead!" her father had shouted, while her mother kept quiet and still. "I have no daughter! As God is my witness! If that harlot crosses my doorstep once more, I will strike her down!" Then he had gone out to a church meeting, leaving her and her silent mother to pack her things.

She had slept on the settee in Mavis's front room for six weeks, till Mavis had suddenly taken a dislike to Errol, and had asked her to leave. Jealousy, Errol had said. But Mavis wouldn't discuss it, just saying that she needed her place to herself, and that it was time they found somewhere else. Finding this room had been like a small miracle, and even though it had taken all the money she had in the Post Office to pay the deposit, she had had such plans when she moved in a month ago.

"What am I going to do?" she asked aloud, rolling over, shading her eyes from the sunglare coming through the high dormer window. "What am I going to do?" She couldn't think of anyone to call, who would advise her. All the people she knew were either ones that knew her parents, or were Errol's friends, or like Mavis, friends from work.

That reminded her, she hadn't phoned work to tell them she wasn't coming in. She would have to get a doctor's certificate or she would lose her job, even though she wouldn't get paid for the time off.

 The thought of work made her feel nauseous. Oh, God! Suppose I can't stand the smell of food? The smell of hamburgers, frying chips, milkshake syrup, seemed to pour out of the walls at her, and she rolled off the bed, wishing she could put her head out of the window, but it was too high. She used the broom to push it open and stood under the cold falling draught of Kilburn air, head back breathing deeply.

The nausea went away leaving her feeling thirsty. She made herself some mint tea, and drank it curled in the one armchair, tears running down her face again. Her mother had always made her mint tea when she felt ill. She thought of calling her mother; but instantly rejected the idea. Her mother never kept anything from her father, and Bev had no intention of giving him the satisfaction of being right.

She went along to the surgery along the High Road the next morning, and registered as a patient. It was ironic really, she thought, as she played slow musical chairs towards the doctor's door; she had been intending to come here to see if he would put her on the pill. She had tried her family doctor but he had refused, and had threatened to tell her father if she went anywhere else, saying that the family planning places always notified the GP. Now of course it was too late, had been even before she moved into her room. And Errol must have known, because she hadn't seen him after the first week, and promises of help with the deposit and the rent had never materialised.

"Miss Jordan, is it?" The doctor spoke to the blotter on his desk.

"Jordee, Beverley Jordee," Bev sat down in the chair on the other side of the desk.

He turned over her new card as if expecting full medical records to appear magically on the other side. When they did not appear he read her name, age, and address carefully.

"And what seems to be the trouble?" he asked, looking at her for the first time, his face and voice devoid of any desire to know.

"I've not been feeling well, and I've had to stay off work, so . . ."

"You don't need to see the doctor for a certificate now, you know," he said brusquely. "Just see the receptionist and she will give you a form to fill in for yourself."

His air of dismissal almost swept her from the room, but Bev found herself gripping the edge of the desk, in order not to be swept out.

"I've been sick in the mornings," she tried a rueful smile; it had no effect. "Mornings, afternoons, and evenings, actually."

"Last monthly period?"

Bev gave him the rough approximation that was all that she had because of the irregularity of her periods before.

He grunted. "Did you bring a sample?" he asked the wall above her head.

"A what?" Did he mean of her sick? Bev wondered.

"A urine sample," he told the blotter exasperatedly. "Collect a sample of urine, first thing in the morning, in a *clean* bottle, and bring it to the surgery. The result should be back in a couple of days; phone the receptionist." He wrote on her new card.

"But the certificate?" Bev asked rather desperately. "What should I put on the certificate?" She couldn't put the real reason, she needed something medical that meant upset stomach or something like that.

He sighed and drew a pad towards him. "When did you last work?"

"Tuesday," Bev said.

"There you are, send the next one in."

Outside, when she looked at the certificate and saw that he had signed her off work for two weeks, Bev nearly cried. How on earth was she going to manage without pay for two weeks?

Since she had one day to go on her weekly tube pass, Bev decided to take the certificate in and try and placate the manager. She decided, as she walked along, that she didn't really mind the doctor's manner. Old Dr. Saville would have had a fit, and her father would have had a real excuse to kill her then. At least this one didn't give a damn whether she was Pastor Jordee's daughter.

She shivered, and walked a bit faster towards the tube station, trying hard to ignore the babies in pushchairs. What was she going to do? Mavis was the only person that she knew well enough, in her new life, to talk to about this. But Mavis was barely speaking to her, and besides, she hated Errol.

So do I! Bev realised, and wanted desperately to be back in the safety of her room, so that she could scream and howl to her heart's content. Then wanted, even more desperately, to go round to Errol's house. To see him, to speak to him.

On the tube, she fantasized. Imagining Errol, holding her tightly in his arms, perhaps his voice breaking with emotion, perhaps a fine tremor in the hand that tenderly wiped away her tears.

*I didn't know!* He would say. *My brother didn't tell me. He's jealous, because you love me, and he's been in love with you all this while.*

By the time she alighted at Leicester Square, Bev had convinced herself that Barry was making trouble between her and Errol; that Errol didn't really know.

I'll go round there after I've seen the manager at work, and if he's not there, I'll write a letter and post it through the letter box. Mark it Personal and Private.

She felt so much better that she swung in through the door of the burger bar; hope filling her, bearing her forward, like a fair wind in a schooner's sails.

The manager took one harassed look at her, and his face sketched a lightening perfunctory smile. "Got a certificate?"

"Yes." Bev held it out.

"Good!" He made no attempt to take it, or even read it. "Okay. You relieve Carol on Till Three; have your break an hour later than usual; and if you make up the extra hour today, we'll say no more about it." All the time he was watching one of the new women mop the floor, and dived off to show her the correct, Company way.

Before she knew it, Bev was changed, and joining the organized chaos behind the counter. Perhaps it was best if she went round to Errol's later anyway. He might have found a job, and not be home. Yes, it would be better to go later on, his brother always went to the pub in the evenings.

With this small and overnourished kernel of hope inside her, Bev found that she could cope with work. Sure, when she had her break, she spent it with her swollen feet propped up on a chair, the window wide open beside her, but no one paid any undue attention to this. True, Mavis popped in, and was momentarily concerned, but went away satisfied by Bev's "First day back!" excuse.

By seven that evening however, Bev was so utterly exhausted that in her thoughts, her high, untidy room, assumed grail-like proportions; attainable only after trial by tube, and stairs. All she wanted was a bath and her bed. Not even her fantasy of a loving Errol was worth trekking backwards and forwards across London, from the West End to Stoke Newington, and then home to Kilburn.

Her ears were ringing by the time she reached her door, and she just made it into her room before she fainted. When she came to, she lay for a long time on the floor, so utterly miserable that she could not even find tears. She dragged herself onto the bed, kicked off her shoes, knelt up to struggle out of her coat, then lay down and drew the cover over her.

When she woke, it was to bright early sunlight, and a knocking on her open door. Bev started up: Errol! It could be Errol!

"Yes!" she called sitting up so quickly that her head spun.

"Are you alright? It's me, Merle, from downstairs. Can I come in?"

Before Bev could think of an excuse, looking rather wildly around the untidy room, Merle had come in.

"You're not alright, are you?" she came and bent over Bev.

"I was too tired last night," Bev sketched a hand at her rumpled jumper. "First day back at work!"

The excuse didn't work with Merle, Bev could see that. Merle straightened, and looked down at Bev. "When did you last have something to eat?"

Bev, fighting the morning bout of her now-daily nausea, lifted a pleading hand.

"Stay there!" Merle had turned briskly away. "Don't get up," she ordered, from the doorway.

She was back within a few minutes, a red mug steaming gently in one hand, and a couple of Rich Tea biscuits in the other. She ignored Bev's faint protests and stood over her while she drank the tea, and ate one of the biscuits.

"Thank you," Bev said finally, handing back the mug to her.

"You'd better see a doctor soon," she said.

"I went yesterday," Bev mumbled.

"And?"

Bev wished she would go away, but couldn't find the words to say so. "I've got to take a sample."

"Hah!" Merle's laugh was totally devoid of amusement. "What for? Any woman could tell him what's wrong with you. They can't even take our word for what's happening to us, inside our bodies, can they? They have to have samples . . . tests ."

On her way to work, later that morning, after dropping off the sample—in an empty pill bottle that Merle located—Bev was uncomfortably aware that she had not thanked Merle properly. She thought of buying her some flowers, or a pot plant, but reasoned herself out of it. One: She could not really afford it. Two: Merle might think that Bev expected her to bring her tea in bed every morning.

The next two days were ordeals to be gotten through somehow, and there was no sign of Merle. Bev made herself a cup of tea, as soon as she got up on the first morning, but it did not ease the queasiness. The next evening she filled a thermos flask with hot water, and placed it next to the bed with a mint teabag ready in a cup. That worked so at least the day did not start with her, head down, over the toilet.

The receptionist's laconic: "Yes, Miss Jordan, your test was positive. Do you wish to make an appointment to see the Doctor?" was no surprise to Bev. She had given up any hope that she wasn't pregnant.

The doctor said: "Yes, you are pregnant."

Then he said: "And the father? Does he know?"

Bev shook her head, and looked down at her hands wrestling with each other in her lap. "He doesn't want to know."

"And your parents?"

Bev just shook her head this time.

"Well, what are you going to do? Have you any idea?"

"I don't know," said Bev, in a voice kept soft, because to speak louder would have revealed her fear and shame; the shame of being unwanted that lay like a cloak about her shoulders. In the romances that she'd borrowed from her friends and read surreptitiously in bed, the coy revelation of a child on the way had always led to incredulous joy on the man's part as he tenderly took the woman in his arms, as if she were a fragile china doll.

"Do you have a job?" the doctor was asking.

"Yes," Bev was glad for even that small affirmative. "I work in a burger bar."

"And have you thought of how you will manage if you have the child?"

"If . . . ?" Bev asked. Surely there was no if about it?

"I could arrange for you to see someone privately." His hand strayed up towards the telephone. "That would speed things up. You've left it rather late, you know."

Bev looked blankly at him, she had no idea what he was talking about.

"For a termination . . ." he looked sharply at her. "An abortion. If you are to have the pregnancy terminated, we will have to move fast. Will the father help financially, do you think? Or your parents?"

"An abortion? I don't have to have the baby?" One of her fighting hands disengaged itself to lay flat on her stomach, almost protectively; while the other flew to her cheek, feeling the warmth of hope flaring there.

"If we can get things arranged pretty smartish," he said.

"Private . . . ? That means I'd have to pay." Hope died. "I don't have any money," Bev said, wishing that she had realised before she paid the deposit on her room.

"No savings?" he said, making it sound like he wasn't really surprised. "Well I suppose we had better go through the motions of trying for an NHS one. But I don't really hold out much hope. You can't even plead interruption of studies; damaged prospects; that sort of thing, can you?" He shook his head, and tapped his pen on her notes. "I don't hold out much hope."

He took some paper out of the wooden stand on his desk and wrote busily for a couple of minutes. Then he sealed the letter carefully in a brown envelope, and pushed it across the desk to her. "Take that along to the hospital today, and make an appointment to see the consultant. Send the next one in."


She met Merle on the landing as she was going laboriously up the stairs that evening.

"You sound puffed out," Merle said. "Come in and have a cup of tea, or at least a sit down. You look as if you've been climbing Mount Everest." She took Bev's arm and drew her into her room, depositing her in a chair.

"Why do you always have to put words to my bad feelings?" It came out before she could stop it.

Merle put her head back round the door of her kitchenette. "It's a talent I have!" she laughed.

" I wouldn't call it a talent exactly," Bev said, but she had to smile.

She put her bag down on the floor beside her, and unbuttoned her coat. Then she looked round the room. It was bigger than hers, full of plants, and there were pictures and photographs stuck all over the walls. Merle had a proper bed, not just a mattress on the floor, and there was a duvet in a bright yellow cover, and lots of matching pillows.

"Did the doctor give you some iron tablets?" Merle called from the other room. "You're probably breathless because you're anaemic." She came back into the room with a tray.

"No, he didn't give me any iron tablets," Bev said.

"What did he give you then?" Merle placed the tray on the table by Bev, handed her a mug of tea, offered her a plate of coconut macaroons.

Bev's hand began to shake so hard that the tea spilled. "He gave me a letter to the hospital." It came out as a grief-stricken wail, surprising and overwhelming her. She had not heard herself make that sort of sound since her gran died. Grief for the death to come, took her, shook her body with deep seismic sobs; touching once again an eight-year-old's grief for her gran's soft warmth; and the firm voice with the power to temper the harsh edicts of her father's religion.

"Can't go to the Saturday morning pictures with your friends: It's ungodly! Can't wear make-up: It's ungodly! Can't have a baby: It's ungodly!" Bev heard her own voice career out of control, shouting, as she pounded one fist against the wooden arm of the chair.

Then strong warm arms were holding her, and she was rocked, cradled, hushed and soothed; as no one had since her gran died, certainly not her cool, silent, withdrawn mother.

"Is that what you want?" Merle asked her softly, strong arms still enclosing her. "What you really want?"

"He said it was the best thing," Bev said into Merle's shoulder.

"Did he really say that?" There was anger in Merle's voice, yet her hands were gentle, stroking Bev's back, smoothing her hair.

"Not in so many words," Bev admitted. "But he asked me how I would manage if I had it, and I didn't have any idea . . ." Little by little she was able to tell Merle exactly what had transpired in the doctor's room, and about her appointment to see the consultant at the hospital in two weeks time.

"But what is it *you* really want?" Merle asked again.

"I don't know!" Bev's hands moved of their own accord, clasping her still flat belly. *"I don't know!"*

"Don't you think that you should take some time to decide?" Merle asked her quietly.

"I haven't *got* time. That's what he said, remember?"

"You've got time," Merle said with certainty. "Up until the minute you go into hospital to have it done, you've got the time and the right to think it out; to decide whether it's what you really want."

"What would you do?" Bev asked.

"I don't know what I'd do, in your position," Merle's voice was calm now, all the anger gone. "But I would want it to be *my* decision; no one else's. Don't ask me to get involved in making the decision with or for you, I won't do it. All I can say is that you owe it to yourself, to think it through, and make your own decisions. Christ! You would take longer to decide on a new dress, than that doctor gave you, this morning. I bet he takes longer to decide which *tie* to wear.

Bev heard footsteps on the stairs. She got carefully out of bed, watching her balance, and wrapped her dressing gown around as much of her as it would cover these days. She patted her belly; eight done, and one to go. It was probably Merle. She was due back about now. She usually called up, but if she was silent today, that was not a good sign. Today was the day she did her road test, to see if she could transfer from being a conductor to a driver.

"Merle . . .?" Bev threw open the door.

"It's me, Baby!" said Errol, standing there in a smart camel coat, driving gloves, and highly polished loafers. "Or should I say: Babies?" He smiled as his eyes slipped down over her swollen belly.

He removed his gloves as he moved toward her, and Bev backed, speechless, one hand going protectively to her belly.

"You're looking good," he said, shrugging out of his coat, and laying it carefully over the chair. "I like your hair in braids: roots, Baby, roots!"

Bev still said nothing, watching his mouth move, smile winningly, while he seemed to use up all the air in her room.

"Barry saw you the other day, and he said you were looking good. And he's right." Another wide easy smile. "There's something about a woman when she's carrying your child."

*"Your child?!"* It came out as a massive shout that tightened her belly, making the baby kick protestingly. "This is *my* child! Nothing to do with you. *Nothing at all!"* Bev swept up his coat and strode out onto the landing. "Get out of my sight!" She hurled his coat over the banisters, down into the stairwell.

There was a shout from Errol, and a rattle in the stairwell as something fell out of his coat pockets. Then he was pounding down the stairs.

"Hey! Watch it!" Merle shouted from further down the stairs. "Bev! Bev?" By the sound of it she was taking the stairs two at a time. "Bev! Are you alright?"

"I'm fine, Merle, fine!" Bev leaned over the rail to call down to her. The front door slammed with a force that reverberated through the house, causing the baby to jump.

Merle paused, breathing hard, on the landing below, and looked up at Bev. "Well, don't celebrate feeling so fine by falling over the banisters! Come down and celebrate with me. I'm feeling pretty good too."

"You passed!" Bev went down the stairs.

"Yeah! Merle threw out her arms and bowed. "How about a cup of tea to celebrate?" She ushered Bev into her room.

"Can I have hot blackcurrant?"

"It's babies that like that stuff, not their mothers!" Merle said, repeating a joke that had begun when Bev's craving for hot blackcurrant cordial became evident.

"I'm no baby!" Bev said, with some satisfaction, as she arranged most of the pillows on the bed to support her back. "That's what Errol called me . . . 'Baby, or should I say: Babies?'" Bev mimicked his smooth tones.

"So you threw him out," Merle gave her her drink, and sat on the end of the bed watching her.

"No, I threw his new coat out!" Bev laughed, one hand going to the baby's kick. "That upset him much more! I don't think he'll be round again."

"Do you mind that?"

"Not one bit!" Bev said.

"Will you still not mind, later on?" Merle persisted.

"You never give me any room, do you?" Bev looked down from those searching eyes.

"Fine gestures are great, in the short run," Merle said, looking soberly down into her mug as if it contained a mirror on time. "But you have to live with the consequences for a long time. Is that worth a moment's satisfaction?"

"Oh, it was worth it believe me," Bev said. "And it wasn't any fine gesture. That was the result of a lot of bad nights. Merle, I have gone from loving him, to hating him, and right out the other side. I don't care if I never see him again."

She looked at Merle, sitting there so contained, staring down into her mug. "You still don't believe I made the right decision about the abortion, do you?" she challenged that calmness.

"Don't tell me what I think," Merle said, looking up at her.

"Well somebody had to be on the baby's side! They all made it so easy, Merle! So easy to get rid of it, as if it was a minor inconvenience. But I knew what they were thinking . . ."

"There you go again!" Merle said.

"Well I *did* know!" Bev's voice rose. "'Just another Black child. We don't want any more of those, do we?'" *Somebody* had to be on the baby's side."

"And who was on your side?" Merle asked.

"You were, I thought," Bev said bitterly, and began to struggle off the bed.

"I was," Merle said, pushing her gently back, "and I still am. What I think doesn't matter. I told you before: It's your decision, and I accept it."

"But I'll never know what you really think, will I?" Bev said wistfully.

"We only ever know what people say, Bev," Merle smiled at her. "We make up the rest to suit ourselves."

"Well, I didn't like what they were saying," Bev admitted, sitting there with her hands clasped round her belly. "So I said: No!—To all of them. The doctors, my father, and Errol."

She reached for her mug, and held it out to Merle, smiling. Merle chinked her mug against Bev's, her smile crinkling the laughter lines round her eyes as they both drank.

# Comparing "Tea in the Wendy House" and "He Said"

In both of these stories, a young unmarried woman discovers she is pregnant. In each case, the reader is invited to sympathize with the woman, but thereafter the readings invited by the two stories are rather different.

In your pairs or groups, talk about your readings of the two stories, saying which you prefer and why. The following questions should then help you to make a closer comparison of the two stories in terms of their construction and ideology. Use the questions as a guide to make brief notes on "He Said" and "Tea in the Wendy House" before sharing your thoughts in a whole class discussion.

What you will need to consider in your discussion is how the stories have been written; what decisions have been made by the writers with regard to plot, characterization, point of view, and so on; and what ideas seem to be at work in the texts. You may be able to identify these ideas as being part of a recognizable school of thought or "position" on particular issues.

1.  **How does each story ask to be read?**

Here you are trying to get at the kind of reading that is encouraged by each story. For example, how are you invited to read the different characters and react to their behavior and the ideas they represent? While "He Said" and "Tea in the Wendy House" are both stories about young women who are pregnant and unmarried, one appears to encourage an optimistic reading of the protagonist's future, the other a pessimistic reading. It may be possible to identify the ideologies—that is, the ideas at work—that underlie this difference.

2.  **Why do the texts invite particular kinds of readings?**

To answer this question, you could begin by considering whether there is (or was?) a "traditional" approach in stories about young, unmarried pregnant women, and, if so, what courses of action would be open to the characters. What, for example, might your expectations be—in a traditional treatment of the subject—of the following?

| Scenario (Part 1) | A young woman discovers she is pregnant by a young man she has been going with for some time. | |
| --- | --- | --- |
| Characters | Young woman's reaction? Her parents' reactions? | Young man's reaction? His parents' reactions? |
| Scenario (Part 2) | A date for the wedding is made. | |
| Characters | Young woman's reaction? Her parents' reactions? | Young man's reaction? His parents' reactions? |

The writers of "He Said" and "Tea in the Wendy House" write both *with* and *against* traditional expectations. Lynn and Graham will marry, but it is Lynn who feels trapped. Errol deserts Bev when she becomes pregnant, but Bev later rejects Errol. Why do the writers choose to have their characters behave in these ways? What effect does it have on the way you are invited to read and view the issues raised?

■ In your pairs or groups, compare the two stories with a traditional treatment in terms of the writer's intentions and the assumptions—about marriage, sexual morality, race, and gender roles—that underlie each text.

| | Traditional | "He Said" | "Tea in the Wendy House" |
|---|---|---|---|
| Writer's intentions | | | |
| Assumptions | | | |

3. **How is the "invitation" to read in certain ways extended?**

To answer this question, you will need to consider factors such as the following:

■ Plot: What happens in each story, and what view of events are readers encouraged to take?

■ Characterization: How are the characters constructed and presented? For example, which characters are we asked to read sympathetically? And how is a sympathetic or unsympathetic reading invited? Lynn's mother, for example, is very supportive of her daughter, and yet the reader is not encouraged to see her very sympathetically.

■ Point of view: From whose point of view are the stories apparently told, and with what effect?

■ Tone: What are the writers' attitudes toward their subject. For example, both Barbara Burford and Adèle Geras are sympathetic to their protagonists and present them as likable young women. However, one protagonist is presented as powerless, the other as finding her own strength. What effect does this have on the tone of each story?

■ Structure: How are the events in each story ordered and related to each other, and with what effect?

4.  **How do you read each of the stories?**

For example, are you as sympathetic to Lynn and Bev as the stories appear to ask the reader to be? Do you agree with the view of events presented in each story? How fully do you accept the endings of each story; optimistic in the case of "He Said" and pessimistic in "Tea in the Wendy House"? Was your reading of "Tea in the Wendy House" changed by reading "He Said"? Or did your reading of "Tea in the Wendy House" affect your expectations of "He Said"?

# References

Bates, H. E. "The Good Corn." *Seven by Five: Stories 1926–61*. London: Michael Joseph, 1963.

Burford, Barbara. "He Said." *The Threshing Floor*. Ithaca: Firebrand, 1987.

burns, joanne. "real land." *Penguin Anthology of Australian Women Poets*. Ed. Susan Hampton and Kate Llewellyn. New York: Penguin, 1986.

Chaplin, Sid. "What Katie Did." *The Leaping Lad and Other Stories*. London: Longman, 1973.

Coolidge, Susan. *What Katy Did: A Story*. Boston: Roberts, 1886.

Geras, Adèle. "Tea in the Wendy House." *The Green Behind the Glass*. London: Hamish Hamilton, 1982.

Gilman, Charlotte Perkins. "Turned." *The Charlotte Perkins Gilman Reader: "The Yellow Wallpaper" and Other Fiction*. Ed. Ann J. Lane. London: Woman's, 1980.

Glaspell, Susan. "A Jury of Her Peers." *Images of Women in Literature*. Mary Anne Ferguson. Boston: Houghton, 1991.

Moorhouse, Frank. "Pledges, Vows and Pass This Note." *Room Service: The Comic Writings of Frank Moorhouse*. Ringwood, Victoria: Penguin, 1985.

Saroyan, William. "The Great Leapfrog Contest." *Best Stories of William Saroyan*. London: Faber, 1964.

Stewart, Marion Rachel. "A Mother's Fondness." *Love You, Hate You, Just Don't Know*. Ed. J. Karavasil. London: Hippo Scholastic, 1978.

Stockton, Russell. "Alone at Last." Unpublished story, 1999.

# About the Authors

Bronwyn Mellor holds a doctorate in education and English from the University of Western Australia. She is the publisher and editorial director of Chalkface Press, which she co-founded in 1987 on returning to Australia from Britain. She taught English in secondary schools in England and worked as a contributory writer and advisory teacher at the English and Media Centre in London. She has also taught in secondary schools in Australia and lectured in university courses in curriculum and English studies.

Marnie O'Neill is a senior lecturer at the University of Western Australia in the areas of English education, language literacy and learning, and teaching and learning. Her research interests include English curriculum studies, curriculum policy and practice, language in education, teaching and learning, classroom studies, gender studies, and gifted and talented education. She has also been a secondary school English teacher, an advisory teacher in English, a chief examiner in English and literature, and, for some years, the editor of the journal of the Australian Association for the Teaching of English, *English in Australia*. The writer of numerous papers, articles, and books, she has co-written texts for secondary students published by Chalkface Press.

Annette Patterson teaches sociology and English in the School of Education at James Cook University, Townsville, Queensland, Australia. Previously, she taught English and literature in high schools from 1976–1989. She also has worked as a member of the Chalkface Press writing team to produce texts for secondary English students. Her research interests include critical reading practices and histories of English education. Her book *Questions of English*, written with Robin Peel and Jeanne Gerlach, is forthcoming from Routledge Press. Currently, she is working on a history of reading instruction from the sixteenth century.

This book was typeset in AGaramond by Electronic Imaging.
The typefaces used on the cover were Trajan, AGaramond, Garamond,
    and Helvetica Narrow.
The book was printed on 60-lb. Williamsburg Offset Smooth by Versa Press, Inc.